Have a Healthy and Happy Retirement

Have a Healthy and Happy Retirement

Dr Michael Apple

Hodder & Stoughton
LONDON SYDNEY AUCKLAND

British Library Cataloguing in Publication Data
A record for this book is available from the British Library

ISBN 0 340 74613 0

Typeset by Avon Dataset Ltd, Bidford-on-Avon, Warks

Printed and bound in Great Britain by
The Guernsey Press Co. Ltd, Channel Isles

Hodder & Stoughton
A Division of Hodder Headline Ltd
338 Euston Road
London NW1 3BH

Contents

CONTENTS

Introduction

If you don't know where you're going, you'll end up someplace else.

Yogi Bera

What does retirement mean to you? Is it excitement, change, opportunity? Or threat, decline and stagnation? This book is to help you think positively about retirement so as to remain active and fulfilled for as long as possible.

Whatever the noise and media hype about the young, the active retired are the true coming generation; real economic and sociological freedom lies with you. And, thanks to earlier retirement, you can expect to enjoy these advantages for many more years than was the case when the majority of people retired exhausted and impoverished after a lifetime of drudgery.

The following figures show what I mean. In 1900 less than 5 per cent of the UK population was aged 65 or above; that had risen to 10 per cent by 1951. By 1981 the figure was 15 per cent and this is projected to stay about the same till around 2010, then rise again.

Though this is an optimistic book, it recognises that happiness also involves effort, sometimes painful effort, and sheer good fortune. Nor have I forgotten that life, especially in later years, is uncertain, complex, irritating and tragic and that the most carefully crafted plans may be swept aside by illness, accident or money problems. I

1

set out strategies to avoid such problems and ways of coping if they happen to you.

And yet just as a book on childcare need not dwell on how a child will make a living in its 40s, there is no reason to dwell on all the uncertain aspects of your retirement, things you may not be able to do anything about. My aim is to help you make the best, the very best of your opportunities during what is increasingly called the 'third age', and for that I shall take an undaunted and positive approach throughout this book. I think there are good grounds for so doing, on the basis of ever-increasing life expectancy, steady improvement in standards of health care and the well-recognised increase in the affluence and financial stability of the older population.

I know that some of those who read this book may have health problems, be estranged from their families, be wondering how to make ends meet; I want to speak to you too. Although I cannot remove your personal difficulties, and it is certainly not my intention to rationalise them away, I shall focus on what you can do and encourage you to do it, or else show you ways to come to terms with a life less perfect than you hoped.

One such important area is preserving any relationships under tension, especially with those who may envy your freedoms in retirement but whose continuing goodwill is essential for your happiness. It is also my strong belief that your satisfaction during retirement will be greatly enhanced by putting something back into society. You are wise by virtue of your experience and I believe that you will feel diminished in some way if you do not use some of that wisdom for the greater good. However, I do not want to cajole or shame you into doing things against your wishes; I am so wary about guilt that there is a whole chapter devoted to handling it.

I have deliberately not defined an age of retirement, but many readers are probably in their late 50s or early 60s. The advice I give is applicable from then, through your late 60s and 70s and even to some degree into your 80s. If there is one message to absorb, it is that your age is what you make it; it is not defined by the number of candles on your birthday cake.

This book is for browsing rather than reading cover to cover and for that reason some information and advice is repeated. Some advice may not appeal to you at all or may be unnecessary in your circumstances, but I hope you will find nuggets that will help you maximise on your contentment through the years ahead.

1

Prime Time

Who doth ambition shun and loves to live in the sun?
Shakespeare, *As You Like It*

Was it for this I uttered prayers,
And sobbed and cursed and kicked the stairs,
That now, domestic as a plate,
I should retire at half-past eight?
Edna St Vincent Millais, 'Grown-Up'

Scenario

Charles and Helen walked briskly to the car, the sounds of congratulations and good luck still ringing in their ears. The retirement party had been fun and moving; so many well-liked colleagues, so many happy and amusing memories. It was exciting to be told by so many people what great opportunities lay ahead, how their life could now begin, the things they'd be able to do at last, the travel, the books, the hobbies. One or two colleagues even seemed a little bitter, envious perhaps. 'I don't know how you'll find the time' was a common theme, along with 'Do things while you can, old man'.

They drove home in comfortable silence, each turning over in their mind the variety of emotions and expectations and looking forward to the first day of freedom.

But that first morning didn't go right; Charles felt uncomfortable in casual clothes on a Monday morning; Helen seemed flustered to find him still at home at a time when she was used to being on her own. The house seemed awfully still, the time passed unusually slowly and there seemed to be, well, so much of it. They had several coffee breaks after trivial tasks. Charles even attempted to tidy up his sock drawer, a task he had been promising himself to do for several decades. Is this what retirement was all about; too much time with too little to fill it?

They drank their fourth coffee of the morning feeling vaguely agitated and on edge; Charles concentrated on polishing his tea-spoon, Helen on teasing a stain out of her napkin. Papers and post, normally read at breakneck speed before dashing for work, lay untouched. And it was only 11.30 a.m. It was Helen who spoke first.

'What we need is a routine. For 40 years our lives have been run to a routine. We can't just sit here waiting for retirement to organise us; we have to organise retirement.' Charles fiddled with a blank piece of paper; he scribbled some headings and as quickly scored them out. He finally appeared satisfied: 'Here,' he said, 'how about this: Life After Retirement: what to do and how to do it?' Helen approved. They had found a new project – life, enjoyment and happiness.

Retirement: An open book or a crumpled page?

Retirement as a period of opportunity is a relatively recent option for most people. Not too long ago, you worked till you dropped or else eked out an impoverished existence once you were no longer capable of working, reliant on whatever few resources you had been able to put by, the goodwill of your family and maybe charity. How things have changed! Improved life expectancy and more affluence mean that retirement is no longer an end but a beginning.

The figures are quite startling: a man who is now 50 can expect to live to 84; a 50-year-old women to 87 (UK figures). This means that you can expect to enjoy at least a couple of decades even after retiring at 65. Many people actually plan to retire much earlier. A combination of improved savings, occupational pension schemes, inheritance and property means that increasing numbers can look forward to a life in retirement well above subsistence level – in fact, often in more affluence than during their working life, because so many costs disappear at the time of retirement.

But this does not just happen automatically after retirement; on the contrary, you must take your life into your hands, perhaps more so than at any other previous time in your life.

Previously you had responsibilities towards:

* Parents
* Teachers
* Children
* Bosses
* Customers
* Clients
* Business associates
* Work colleagues.

Do this, fix that, research this, let me do that. Wasn't it dire! Now you are answerable just to yourself. Well, not totally; the web of family, friends and other unavoidable commitments will still restrain your total freedom. But at last you are the one mainly in charge of your agenda and this is not an agenda for organising the staff car park but for life. No one will force what you do. If you want to spend your time day-dreaming, that's now up to you. Or fall into a comfortable, unthinking routine of shopping and housework, that's up to you too.

But you are looking beyond this, otherwise you wouldn't be reading this book. So you want something more; retirement for you is excitement and opportunity. And you are lucky enough to be among the first few generations of humankind who can make that new beginning with health, energy, affluence and fantastic opportunities for physical, mental and social growth. This is tremendous, but it is also a little frightening at first. We humans are creatures of pattern and routine, forever trying to impose order on a frustratingly disordered universe. We moan about routine and complain of getting bored with it; but take routine away and most of us feel exposed.

This is natural. So it is entirely understandable that when you look into retirement and old age you may see:

- Emptiness
- Uncertainty
- Debility
- Decline.

No one can deny that these may happen. But rather than submit to such negative emotions, consider how to transform them through planning and forethought. Then you get:

- not emptiness but a programme of activities
- not uncertainty but an anchor in time and place
- not debility but a programme for fitness
- not decline but forward planning for the possibility of dependency.

This is why in later chapters I am so keen to suggest ways of organising yourself and taking charge of that agenda of life.

Ageism; why it matters and why attitudes are changing

The ageism I have in mind is not the dry, politically incorrect dogma you read about; leave that to the political activists. The ageism I mean is the internalised, self-imposed ageism which thinks: because my birth certificate says I'm 65 I'm sure going to act 65. And the day I turn 70 I'll buy myself a rocking chair and ease up. If you think about it, these commonly expressed ageist views are actually very curious; you don't take this attitude with a car, you don't even do it with a toaster. You look at the age, of course, but you also look carefully at the condition; that is to say, how effectively it will do what it's meant to do. Why? Because condition is the best guide to future performance, not age alone. This is a crucial difference. It is the difference between chrono-logical age, i.e. time from birth, as opposed to biological age, i.e. the way you have aged compared to the average. This is the truth behind the saying that you are as old as you feel, which is no less true for being so familiar. We can also call this apparent age (AA) as opposed to chronological age (CA).

Ageism is an attitude that implies that apparent age and chronological age must be the same. The equation goes $AA/CA = 1$. This is pure moonshine. We can all think of people who seem much older than they really are; they look wrinkled, act slowly and are resistant to change. Their age quotient goes something like: apparent age 70, chronological age 50, age quotient $70/50 = 1.4$.

Then again there are those – like you, I hope – whose apparent age is much less than their chronological age. Let's say that you compare yourself with a 55 year old, though your chronological age says you are 65. $AA/CA = 0.85$ (approx). That's a figure I like, something below 1. Now for this exercise to be valid, you must be honest with yourself. You must throw away those rose-tinted glasses. For example, your skin is unlikely to escape ageing; you will have liver spots and skin blemishes. But exercise, tolerance, vision, stamina, memory, understanding – these may all compare very well indeed with people chronologically equal to you in age or younger.

Why is ageism, as we have defined it, important? Because if you think of yourself as old, you subconsciously come to accept the ageist attitudes of others. Try as you may, you all too easily see yourself through their prejudiced eyes and think yourself into an age that bears little relationship to the way you really feel on any objective measures of physical and mental fitness. Before you know it, you are telling yourself to behave years older than you feel; subconsciously your body language alters to reflect this imaginary age. And, surprise, surprise, others pick up on this and start treating you older than you wish. One day, it is true, someone will give up their chair for you and you will accept it with relief. But you want that to happen at the appropriate time and not while you still feel fit enough to be planning a trekking holiday to the Himalayas.

New freedoms – getting to feel comfortable

Welcome to your liberated life. Your freedoms are in:

- **Time:** Your time is now mainly yours to organise.
- **Space:** Freedom to travel or not to travel, freedom to move home

or take up temporary residence depending on interests, hobbies and emotional ties.

- **Personal growth:** You can opt for new interests, build on old ones. The public persona so long necessary in your work or your social position may now be changeable.
- **Emotion:** It is less comfortable to acknowledge that you may feel free to reassess long-standing emotional attachments and relationships.

How to start

These freedoms can crowd in on you in the first flush of retirement. The reaction can go either way: a retreat into the status quo or a frenetic process of change and self-reinvention that risks leaving a cruise ship's wake of emotional debris. The sensible way is to test out some relatively minor non-threatening freedoms while thinking deeply about the more major ones. Ideally you will have given some thought to the major implications well before you retire (see Chapter 3, 'How to Plan Ahead'). So enjoy the freedom of a lie-in on what for others is a working day, of having breakfast in the garden while waving happily to those setting off on their journey to work. A film in the afternoon, a coffee in town, a leisurely lunch, the pleasure of having the car serviced without worrying about your schedule, or at last seeing just what the gasman does to maintain your system and to justify the bill you have always resented. You may take the journey to your place of work, relishing the atmosphere and seeing with leisurely eyes the route previously dulled by familiarity. But whatever you do, it isn't wise to visit work immediately, because that could raise uncomfortable emotions and conflicts.

In such small ways, explore your reaction to your new freedom and get comfortable with the feeling. You should especially try things that make you feel really guilty even to think about. It may be going to the cinema in the afternoon, spending a morning in the library, surfing the Internet. It may be throwing out all the papers relating to your work. The more guilt it raises the better, because one of the first things you need to get out of your system is feeling guilty about your new situation. Relish that slight edge of apprehension at being caught out. Imagine your boss, a client or a customer seeing you now: no other explanation is necessary other than the sheer self-indulgence of what you are doing. In a sense, relish the guilt, confront it and get used to it; you can do whatever you want without having to justify yourself to others.

Goodbye to routine

Congratulations on slipping off the restrictions of routine. Now, whatever routines you follow can be of your own making; whatever deadlines you set reflect your personal priorities, not someone else's. Your day and your week will take on a wholly different structure. Once, your week was set out as a grid of allocated times, underlined targets, competing options, unending priorities – a more or less threatening diary which said: Do it! Now, your week will lose its sharp edges, beginning, of course, with the rigid demarcation between weekend and working week, between playtime and serious time.

The boundaries are no longer imposed by external forces except in the most obvious sense that Saturday is still Saturday and time-tables of transport, shopping and leisure are still relevant. But previously a schedule drove you; now you set the schedule, based on your requirements alone. Weekends may actually become your preferred time to retreat from society and the crowds of weekend shoppers or theatregoers. You may prefer to use your weekends for 'housekeeping', when you do jobs around the house, the bills, the maintenance, the correspondence, leaving others to their quick burst of freedom.

In other words, how you choose to define your week or your day depends much less on external requirements and much more on your personal priorities. In a way, time expands for you and becomes more fluid, passing quickly over the less enjoyable tasks and more slowly over your preferred activities.

Similarly for those other factors – space, emotions, personal growth. Again there will still be certain fixed points of reference; a journey of 200 miles is still a journey that has to be planned, and obligations to friends and partners remain important – in some ways more important. Your freedom from imposed routine means that your planning for such factors can be based on an emotional time-table rather than one driven purely by time. So a long journey need no longer be something squeezed in among your other commitments; rather, it can become an end in itself, the journey being part of the experience. Why take a motorway, when you now have the leisure to take a secondary road? Why speed from smoky and expensive service station to service station when you can move from village café to village café?

So too for matters of emotion; the journey becomes part of the experience. No longer constrained to socialise briefly, you at last have the time to explore relationships more deeply than before. Casual acquaintances may now prove to be more interesting than you thought; old friends may have aspects to their characters you have never realised. Your own husband, wife or partner will show a different side when your spheres of interaction expand to include most of the day rather than only part.

Beware – this is a tricky time. There is a very real risk that a friendly relationship that works fine for three hours a fortnight will wilt under the attention of two hours a day. In pursuit of your own emotional requirements you may unwittingly be imposing your agenda on someone else, making life as uncomfortable for them as when others imposed their agendas on you. The key is sensitivity, allowing space, making suggestions rather than fixing plans, and growing towards a mutually agreeable exposure rather than moving too quickly to regular but empty meetings.

But not totally free . . .

Enjoy this new-found freedom for the wonderful opportunity it is; the opportunity to look within yourself in order to decide what will be most important for you in the future. This has probably been a rare sensation hitherto; even holidays and leisure activities carry an undertone of deadlines and endpoints that inevitably colour the total enjoyment. It is a natural temptation to throw routine to the winds, to consign your diaries to the dustbin and your e-schedules to the recycle bin, and donate your personal electronic organiser to a worthy, obsessional, time-constrained home – a tax inspector might do.

A wiser course would be to make some satisfying symbolic gestures, because you cannot totally escape from routine. By all means throw out your diaries – but keep one back. Enter 'free time' all over your electronic time management system, but don't delete the program. Let your friends know you are available for lunch, golf, walking or just meeting whenever they wish, but if you do, expect conflicting arrangements sooner than you might think.

Enjoy being a free spirit, summoned wherever and whenever Life chooses. For a few weeks or months Life will be exhilarating, fresh, ever surprising. Fun. However, be prepared soon for some vertigo, as if you were looking over a cliff top and for similar reasons. Without some frames of reference you can easily lose your bearings and find your freedom more unsettling than exciting. All too easily your activities become driven by whim and chance in ways that can feel threatening and uncomfortable. How much of a problem this is for you depends on your personality and your tolerance of uncertainty; it may not bother you personally. Most people, however, welcome some degree of organisation and routine in their lives as a way, paradoxical as it may seem, of enhancing their sense of freedom and use of time.

As an example, consider basic 'housekeeping' activities such as shopping, housework, dealing with finances and seeing relatives. It is possible to do these activities on an ad hoc basis as and when the need arises. Indeed, for many retired people shopping seems to have become an end in itself and a major part of their activity. If this describes you, read no further.

But it could make more sense to organise your week so that you have definite shopping days, perhaps with top-up days as necessary. Knowing, for example, that Tuesday morning is your day for shopping will impose a gentle healthy routine. You will budget to have the money available, keep an eye on what is needed and buy enough for the week, or whatever period of time you choose. You can add social activities, meeting people, lunches, etc., to your shopping trip, and at the same time you might decide about clothes, cleaning and other mundane but essential affairs. Thus you will fit into, say, three hours a week activities which might take much more time if done in dribs and drabs.

Shopping is obvious, but how about other matters? Such as reviewing finances? You may decide to review your bank statement and budget monthly and take an overall look at your finances twice a year. If seeing friends on a regular date can become an empty routine, where it is mutually agreeable there is a lot to said for arranging a regular meeting, to plan definite joint outings and activities.

Nature abhors a vacuum; in retirement you are the vacuum that other people may try to fill and you should be aware of the risk. Their motives may be benign; they may think they are doing you a favour in filling what they suppose is your otherwise empty time. How easy it is to become the babysitter for grandchildren, the dutiful child who always checks on an elderly parent, the good neighbour who runs errands for others. This may not be a problem for you; it may be a great pleasure; but at times even the pleasure can be blunted by a sense of being taken for granted. Having your own routine is a way to regulate this possibly unwelcome creeping occupation of your own time by others, however well meaning. In this respect it is useful to be able to say 'On Tuesdays I always . . .' or 'Friday is my regular day for . . .' so that others get the hint that you have your own personal requirements and that you are not entirely at their disposal.

You may want to have a lifestyle that requires longer-term planning, such as spending part of the year abroad or taking holidays at regular intervals. On the one hand retirement offers the benefit of doing things at short notice, such as taking a holiday; on the other, opportunities can come and go and are missed precisely because you failed to prepare in advance.

So you are unlikely to be able to escape routine entirely. The trick is to select routines that benefit you rather than submit to routines that rule your life. Within this framework there are bound to be less agreeable routines – relatives who must be seen, meetings or obligations flowing from organisations to which you belong. It may seem odd to welcome such constraints into what should be a time of pleasure and freedom, but a completely obligation-free existence can encourage a selfish, self-centred attitude which could lead you into a crabby, irritable old age – which is not the plan at all.

Coping with family and friends

You may have dreamed of the look of envy and irritation from friends and family when you announce your retired status. It is easy to imagine their reaction; just think how you have felt when your friends and relations have gloated over their own retirement; it may not be wise to go on about it too much. Be prepared for comments on how much time you will have, how lucky you are to have the money to retire early. There will be cautionary tales about so-and-so who only enjoyed a few weeks of leisure before contracting such and such an illness and there will be commiserations for your partners and children living at home 'who will have to put up with you more now'.

Underlying such comments is their understandable, genuine uncertainty about what lies ahead for you and how that may affect their relationship with you. It is, after all, a truism that how we relate to others very much reflects their status, which in turn largely reflects their occupation and all that flows from it. Occupation is an easy, convenient way of categorising people, as useful for close relations as it is for less intimate friends (see next section).

You should also realise that at the moment of retirement you crystallise, as it were, into what can understandably be seen as your final shape in terms of what you have achieved in life, love, endeavour, power, money, experiences, woes and happiness. Try not to let this crystallisation ensnare you, because in your own mind retirement is not an end but a beginning. While you realise this within yourself, your friends and family may need convincing. They think you will continue as you were at the point of retirement, but with more leisure and altered finances. You may feel comfortable with that route, but hopefully your horizons will be more extensive, more demanding, less routine.

Understanding their point of view helps you to reinterpret the well-meaning remarks made by your friends and relatives, because they are speaking to themselves as much as to you. They are reassuring themselves that you will remain the same, because to think otherwise is to accept the uncertainty you now represent. Will your relationship change; will your interests remain the same, the depth of your friendship as profound, the extent of affection as strong, and your attachment as reliable . . . ?

You could play some mind games to get them a little unsettled. Hint at how all options are fluid and all routes open to exploration, at how you are re-evaluating your life and where you go from here. Do this to unsettle if you wish, but also to see the response it generates. You may find that close friends have insights into your strengths or aspirations that you don't see or have forgotten about.

So use family and friends as sounding boards; you may be surprised to learn that they think you could follow directions you had over-looked.

Games aside, here is a time to genuinely re-evaluate your relation-ships. Relationships take more effort than most of us have during our working life. Now may be the time to deal with shortcomings in how you have related to those close to you, to explain oversights and relive memories. This could get maudlin, looking at the haunts of your youth over bottles of wine. That is not at all the idea, because too much recollection will prevent you from moving forward. Rather, acknowledge those shared experiences, which bond you together, as a way of reinforcing the foundations of your relationship before taking the next steps forward. This is as important for your loved ones as it is for yourself, because it reassures them that you are not going to grow away from them. The last thing you want at the time of retirement is to lose your loved ones just as you have to cope with all the other changes in your situation.

How to respond to others

Just as you are seeking to readjust, so you will be the subject of readjustment. If your partner retires at the same time as you, they will be going through a similar process of re-evaluation and may conclude that you do not hold the same position in their own priorities. Uncomfortable, yes? A period of mutual wariness is likely. In order to make this easier, keep talking. Here are some important topics to discuss:

- How you intend to spend your time
- Allowing each other space, physical and emotional
- Allocating responsibilities between you – finances, shopping, housework, holiday planning, etc.
- Any tensions and difficulties that need sorting out
- What you each expect of each other.

Just how much this applies to you and yours depends on how open and mutually supportive your relationships were before retirement. You are likely to continue as you have before; if that was a relation-ship of simmering resentments, retirement is likely to throw these into greater relief; if it was one where you could acknowledge and work on problems, then this aspect of retirement should be easier to handle.

Job, work, status

You're great ...

It is generally held that your job defines who you are, the worrying implication being that when you stop work you enter a social vacuum. How are people supposed to judge you now? This greatly concerns people facing retirement, especially those whose jobs carry significant authority and, even more so, those who have doubts about their own natural authority, charisma or whatever. It may come as a surprise to know that this will include many people in senior positions. Why? Because we all know that life is not a smooth progression where the ablest rise effortlessly. More often it is an interaction of chance and ability, drawing on natural aptitudes but much more subject to the unexpected than people care to admit.

The vigorous chief executive or the worthy senior partner may both owe their position more to chance promotions than that the world recognised their superior abilities. Conversely, for those many millions of us carrying out the routine jobs that any society needs, who is to say how life might have gone for us with different education, family opportunities, etc? What if the boss had visited our office on the day we were performing spectacularly well; how might our promotion have gone?

It is goodbye to all that; the trappings of achievement, the networks and the subtle social supports that both make and maintain anyone's social standing. Now what?

You can be greater

Daunting as such a loss may seem, there is another way of looking at it. Because here is the chance to reinvent yourself, free of those obligations which have kept you on a more conventional path hitherto. Life no longer has to include a business suit or work overalls.

You are no longer 'Mrs Bacon of Housing' or 'Mr Smith of Supplies'. That same stereotype which, let us be frank, supported and comforted you over the years, can now be abandoned like a caterpillar shedding its skin. And in abandoning that, you are abandoning the expectations that others had of you, expectations which, like it or not, moulded your behaviour because you tended to conform to the stereotype. 'Mr Smith of Supplies; oh yes, good on detail but hopeless at seeing the big picture'; 'Mrs Bacon of Housing; watch her, she gets upset if you don't fill in the form perfectly.' Is this you? Was this you? What does it matter? It no longer need be you.

Growth with wisdom

The changes you can make at this stage in your life come with a built-in advantage; you are building on your own history, self-knowledge, self-value, vision. Unlike the comi-tragic self-invention of teenagers or those struggling to find themselves in adult life, you can move forward with the knowledge of who you already are. You may or may not be satisfied with how your life has gone, but, as a thinking adult, you will understand your place in the world and should be able to bring to mind solid, definite achievements which have made a difference to others.

Being yourself

Now comes the difficult but rewarding part. You have left behind restraints of status, work, income, etc. You stand, apprehensively perhaps, at a new beginning. Your future is in your own hands to a degree you have not enjoyed up to now. So where next? Are you completely free? The answer to that is no, not entirely. Though you can expect a remarkable degree of freedom, there are some fundamental truths you will have to acknowledge. You will be able to look back at achievements, but you would be a truly exceptional person if you have really achieved everything you hoped for in life. Behind you there will be opportunities missed, decisions fudged, relationships unfulfilled.

You could brood about all this and relive your life as it might have been if you had got everything right. That may be an interesting diversion for one summer afternoon; but it is not fruitful as a basis for your future health and happiness. You have to learn to abandon what has been, without losing any of the personal growth those experiences have given you. Those unique experiences have made you yourself, the disappointments as well as the achievements, but it is unhelpful to keep reviewing them.

Not complacent...

This is not say that you should accept yourself 'warts and all'. That is a self-satisfied conclusion which does not allow room for improvement. Rather, your aim should be to say, 'I am as I am; this is why and this is where I am going'.

There is a useful phrase that sums this up; aim to have bottom. Not *a* bottom – for dealing with that see the section on exercise. 'Having bottom' means that your personality is set on a firm basis that includes self-esteem, self-knowledge, self-awareness and the confidence in your own opinion that flows from that. Once again, this is so different from the cockiness of youth, which is based on nothing more than confidence without, as yet, anything behind it – which is why it is jarring to older people who see how life really goes. What you are aiming for is the confidence that flows from a sense of your own worth derived from having real, as opposed to potential, achievements. Knowing this, you are in a position to decide how to progress without running counter to those fundamental aspects of your personality which you realise will rule out certain options.

Here is an example. You're retired? A friend tells you that you must take up bridge. Thirty years earlier you might have thought. 'Yes, I must, because everyone tells me I must or else I'll have a boring retirement.' Now you say: 'Thanks for the advice, but I can't stand card games and I know I never will. Why don't you join me in taking up tennis?'

This sounds simple, even banal. But it is actually rather difficult to confront what many will regard as received wisdom and to take your own advice.

How to make a fresh start

This is entirely optional; there is absolutely nothing about your stage of life that forces you into recreating yourself; indeed, it is part of your maturity to avoid doing so against your wishes. However, for reasons shown earlier, you may feel that now is the moment to begin afresh, as it were, to fulfil those unfulfilled aspirations for which you still have the motivation, the energy and, most crucially the time.

This is tremendously exciting, even a little scary, because of the enormous opportunity. When else in your life have you been able to take your destiny into your own hands so decisively? Certainly not as a child, definitely not as a teenager – though we all remember the sense of an open future that we felt in those teenage years when everything seemed possible and every path seemed open. But, in reality, chances are you were overtaken by those dull realities of job, career, education, obligations and money.

As an adult, your life was restrained in all the ways discussed earlier. So now really is the time, if this is what you want. You still need to balance those obligations that you can't avoid – family, partners, friends. Before you go totally changing your life you owe these loyal others due care and attention. Think to yourself, would you stay friends with yourself if you were quite different from the way you have been for many years?

Therefore my advice is to think big, but start small. It may be as simple as changing a favourite jacket for something daringly more modern; perhaps a range of shirts or blouses in colours other than that old favourite, 'safe for work'. Seeing a film you might not have considered, reading a magazine that has absolutely nothing to do with homemaking, visiting a town you've always wanted to see and never got round to. Enjoy the sensation of novelty, spontaneity, freshness. Then ponder the next steps: the hobbies you might consider, the travels you might make, new challenges, new people. Talk these over with your friends for a bit of reality testing – because you still need that. Then turn to the chapter on planning ahead, and enjoy.

How to analyse your abilities

A SWOT analysis is a simple tool, much used in business, that will help you to focus on yourself. SWOT stands for Strengths, Weaknesses, Opportunities, Threats. You may feel a little foolish doing this – after all, who needs business tools at your age – yet you will be surprised at how useful it is in summarising your situation.

Strengths
Put down the 10 things about yourself that you have found most useful in making your way through life and through relationships. They should be things you feel comfortable with, where you believe you have had success. Examples might include 'good at detail', loyalty, stamina, can tell jokes, decisive.

Weaknesses
These are things that others have probably mentioned or which you may have decided on as a result of self-examination. A good test is whether you feel embarrassed at even writing them down privately. Not so easy this one. You may wish to hide this from others, but try to be honest. Weaknesses might include short-tempered, lazy, poor personal hygiene. List a maximum of 10.

Opportunities
Here list 10 things you feel you could achieve. Make some short-term goals such as renewing your wardrobe and other longer-term goals such as getting fit, or travelling. Note that these are not quite the same as aspirations; rather, they are ways in which you can build on your strengths or correct your weaknesses.

Threats
Here, list 10 things which significantly hamper your freedom to plan. Examples might be income, disability and obligations to others.
  Categorise items as:

- Possible to change
- Possible to change but difficult
- Impossible to change.

Put these lists aside for a few days, then see whether you wish to alter or add to them. Now you have a summary of your situation. What next?

You need to review this summary to see what is important for you. Those things you can do nothing about you have to live with; thus a goal of travel might be compromised by needing to look after elderly parents. However, once you have things written down in this way, you should be able to see more easily how you can achieve your goals or deal with your problems than if you carry everything in your head in an unordered way. Try it and see for yourself.

A SWOT analysis is not a solution but a framework for making sense of your path ahead. It may not appeal to you; you may not be the sort of person who analyses situations in this way and may feel that you are more spontaneous. That's fine too; that is in fact your particular strength – to make the most of situations as they arise. For many others, having so many options all at once, as one does after retirement, can feel overwhelming unless they impose some sort of order on things. I suggest that even the most spontaneous of readers will still have talked over the future with friends and partners, so why not try a SWOT analysis just for fun?

Case study

Charles and Helen looked at the blank piece of paper labelled SWOT; they felt somewhat silly; the sun was shining and they could be outside gardening or visiting a neighbour or perhaps putting up a shelf. There were so many things to do it was difficult to know where to start. Grinning wryly at each other, they realised that that was precisely the problem. A SWOT analysis was perhaps not so bizarre after all. They agreed to write theirs individually and to compare notes afterwards and they said they would each try to be honest – difficult, that bit. A blank piece of paper, memories of a well-spent life, anticipation of an interesting future – it was a small investment of time compared with what they hoped would be a long future, and beat cleaning the vegetable rack by a long way.

They found that several of their assessments differed; in a variety of areas they were stronger (or weaker) than they thought. Each felt that they had important opportunities that had to be co-ordinated with their partner to avoid clashes between, for example, a wish to move house and a wish to travel. It took some while to think this over but at the end they had much better agreement about planning for the future and a much clearer idea about their important goals in retirement.

Fear no more the frown of the great, thou art past the tyrant's stroke.
Shakespeare, Cymbeline

2

How to Analyse
Where You are At:
A Section Reviewing Your
Starting Position

Life is not a rehearsal.

John Lennon

Anyone retiring at, say, 60 can expect about 25 years of life ahead of them; your immediate aim is to make that remarkable quarter century as productive and fulfilling as possible. In order to do so, I suggest that you should have as clear an idea as possible of your starting position; if you know where you are starting from, you are more likely to make a success of arriving at where you want to be.

Just how far you go down this route is an individual choice; so too is how detailed you wish to make the process. Some people feel that the very essence of retirement is not to plan and schedule as you did in your working life. Now is the time to let life wash over you and to enjoy a more spontaneous existence, freed from the constraints of timing and conflicting demands. Is this you? If so, you have probably already booked the flights to your desert island and ordered the food and drink. Everyone should enjoy this type of experience and relish the sheer pleasure of doing things on whim, at the spur of the moment and in a rush of enthusiasm.

Most of us prefer more order in our lives, though always with us setting the rules rather than the rules running us. Think again of that 25-year retirement span and relate that to, for example, bringing up your children, or pursuing your career or developing your home. How much of those processes did you actually leave to pure chance? It would be surprising if you had not set yourself certain goals and tried to keep things on course in a broad sense, while still coping with the uncertainty that life hurled at you along the way.

Even as simple a schedule as, let us say, painting the house every five years, or keeping an eye on the central heating once a year. That would hardly strike you as an oppressive planning process, but rather a sensible ordering of priorities that made sense of other aspects of your life such as savings, the type of savings, access to funds for the unexpected, budgeting for the inevitable. That is all I am suggesting at this stage in your life and you will be surprised at what a comfort it is to know that there is a plan to what might otherwise seem a dauntingly unstructured period of time.

Just for fun, see what type of person you are.

		Yes	No
Do you file credit card statements		3	0
You keep your car tidy		1	0
You file holiday photos immediately		3	0
You have a hammock in the garden		1	0
You throw out food after its sell-by date		2	0
Your socks are:	More than 75% matched	3	
	50–74% matched	−1	
	Under 50% matched	−3	

Score
Add all yes answers and deduct any minus score.

9–13   You are organised and probably feel uncomfortable with uncertainty.
0–8   You keep a balance between spontaneity and regulation.
Any minus score: Oh dear. . .

Human needs and aspirations

The psychologist Abraham Maslow suggested a hierarchy of human needs and aspirations. His view was that 'higher' aspirations become important to an individual only when more basic priorities have been satisfied. His classification may not be fully comprehensive but it is a useful means of structuring human aspirations and their order of priority. Here it is.

Physiological needs: Food, shelter, warmth, sex.

Safety needs: Insecurity, threats to well being, health, fear, stability.

Social needs: Love and acceptance within a social framework such as a family, a group, religion.

Esteem needs: These are such things as respect and self-confidence and flow very much from your perceived position in the eyes of others.

Self-fulfilment needs: These satisfy deep-seated psychological urges that may not even be apparent until the four previous levels have been satisfied. They may include urges to explore, to create, to find power, seek truth, beauty, justice.

Though Maslow proposed these as a hierarchy of needs, in reality the order is by no means this rigid. In some individuals, for example, their drive to self-fulfilment, justice or creativity may override their needs for esteem from others or even lead them to neglect basic health and security needs. These individuals 'live for their job' or 'drive themselves into the ground'. But as a broad generalisation, Maslow's categorisation provides a sound way of assessing ourselves and others. When we talk of someone losing a sense of proportion, for example as a workaholic, we recognise that they are letting one level of needs thrive at the expense of more basic needs.

Maslow's categorisation is particularly appropriate to the affluent society we are fortunate enough to enjoy, because the converse of his categorisation says that you can hardly worry about self-esteem if you are still struggling to get enough to eat. Our own century provides examples of how previously civilised, self-fulfilling societies have degenerated into satisfying more basic needs as the social organisation has crumbled or became distorted.

A needs assessment

NEEDS	Score 1 (least)–5 (best)
Satisfaction with housing	
Access to food, transport	
Overall state of health	
Do you feel comfortable?	
How good a social life?	
Do you see your family?	
Do you feel needed and loved?	
How do you rate your self-worth?	
Has your life been fulfilled so far?	
How optimistic do you feel about the future?	
TOTALS	

Assessment

0–24: You have serious deficiencies in your lifestyle that require careful review. There are fundamental problems you need to recognise and address.

25–36: On the whole your situation is satisfactory; there are pockets of unmet need you should review.

37–50: Congratulations; your life sounds well planned and in keeping with your aspirations. Your goal is not to become complacent about your achievements.

Ideally these are the sort of assessments to make well in advance of retiring, when your income allows you to get your home and money matters in order and you are in an established lifestyle. If the prospect of retiring fills you with gloom rather than anticipation, it is worth reviewing your situation in the light of Maslow's scheme. It may be that there are fundamental needs that you have not properly addressed, such as housing and finances. Or your social situation may be unsatisfactory. The scheme does not give answers, but it does help you to focus in an organised way on assessing your current standing.

How relationships can affect decision-making

Part of the process of planning should include an assessment of where you stand in relation to the 'significant others' in your life – partners, family. Where relationships are good, your happiness intertwines with their happiness; where relationships are bad, you may feel able to ignore how seeking your own satisfaction will affect others. Here again it may be useful to draw up a simple table of relationships and how you rate them. For example:

Relationship	Poor (0–3)	Fair (4–7)	Good (8–10)	Change desired? Likelihood
Partner				
Children				
Parents				
Main friends				
Acquaintances				
Ex-colleagues				
Others				

This gives a basis of scoring and helps prioritise changes. There is no right or wrong score; this is more a snapshot of your relationships. Lots of 'poors' call for soul-searching. In general, prioritise dissatisfactions in relation to the first four headings, as it is on these relationships that your happiness will mainly depend. Be prepared to spend time analysing these relationships and, where they are unsatisfactory, in deciding where this dissatisfaction lies.

Difficulties unresolved during your working life are more likely to be resolved after retirement, when you have more time and your aspirations or competing demands become easier to reconcile. It would be comforting, but wrong, to think that resolving means reconciliation; this is by no means the only outcome. You may feel that certain relationships are no longer worth the effort; that they have been kept alive only through obligation, custom and guilt and cause too much heartache (or give too little reward) to be worth maintaining. In the chapter on guilt there are suggestions for dealing with these situations.

Needs, wants and aspirations

In order to reach a comfortable assessment of your starting position, it may be helpful to make a distinction between these concepts.

- Need: a condition marked by the lack or restraint of some necessary thing
- Want: a lack of something desirable
- Aspiration: a desire for something at present above you.

Needs

In general an unfulfilled need leaves you feeling physically uncomfortable (for example cold, hungry), because needs tend to be the more fundamental things in life (the first two categories of Maslow's hierarchy). There may be health issues you have yet to address – a painful hip, breathlessness. Or perhaps you have been too rushed up to now to follow a proper diet or change your car. Most needs are relatively simple both to identify and to satisfy. There can be no excuse in our society to miss out on satisfying the basic needs of food, shelter, health and companionship.

Wants

A want leaves you feeling mentally unhappy through being denied something you feel you should have. Common wants include more money, looking better, a newer car, a different neighbourhood and more leisure. Wants tend to involve Maslow's higher categories, even verging on self-fulfilment; in a materialistic society possessions may substitute for more spiritual self-fulfilment.

Our society puts much emphasis on satisfying material wants; there is no denying the pleasure that comes from owning good things seen to their best advantage. However, maturity brings an understanding that material possessions do not necessarily provide contentment or happiness. By retirement many people have reached a level of material possessions which is likely to be the maximum they will either want or achieve. It makes sense, therefore, not to dwell too bitterly on those possessions (wants) you have not achieved because this will leave you feeling envious and resentful.

Such destructive emotions could interfere profoundly with your mental satisfaction during retirement. So, in assessing your wants, try to dwell not on those which realistically are out of your reach – the yacht, the jewellery, the house, and identify instead those which you are more likely to be able to fulfil – the makeover, the hobby, the new car, the new social groups.

This is not to say that there will be no more goals to attain or achievements to fulfil; of course there are. What I am suggesting is that you apply a mature judgement about what is likely to be achievable rather than become fixated on what has eluded you up to now and is likely to elude you in future.

Aspirations

Missing an aspiration may cause anything from a momentary disappointment to a profound sense of worthlessness in your life. Few of us can look back on a life that has met all our aspirations; be very suspicious of anyone who says they can. Along the way there are bound to have been missed opportunities, personal gifts not fully explored, opportunities misunderstood at the time or botched.

Our own assessment of our worth almost always runs way ahead of our true abilities, so in a sense everyone's life can be a disappointment, if that is how you choose to see it. This is why it is so important to recognise what you have achieved and to congratulate yourself.

Actually, do more than congratulate, really give yourself a big ovation for surviving the twentieth century. We may no longer live in a life or death society, struggling to exist, but there remain disillusionment, guilt, self-reproach and hardship. It takes a quiet dedication to have got through life in the twentieth century, to have survived and thrived under its enormous social changes, some terrible conflicts and the ever-accelerating pace of change in the last 25 years. Maybe you didn't wrestle with tigers, climb tall buildings or catch speeding bullets with your bare teeth. But you ran the store, made the accounts balance; you improved a widget, invented a thingummy, and turned aimless infants into tolerable members of society. You mended your fences, said hi to your neighbours, voted often, and made some people laugh. You are a hero!

Boost your self-esteem, therefore, by concentrating first on how well you have dealt with your basic needs. Once you have that straight in your head, look carefully at your aspirations. Paradoxically, you may then find that what you had thought were needs/wants actually become less important in the light of understanding your true aspirations. You may have to go round in these circles a couple of times to arrive at a final assessment of your situation. It is worth doing this, because it will be in trying to satisfy your aspirations that you will derive the most happiness in your retirement

Write an end-of-term report about yourself

Here are some possible headings:

- Physical condition
- Home comforts
- Relationship with person closest to you
- Relationships with friends
- Relationships with family
- Financial standing
- Satisfaction with life to date
- Self-knowledge

- Skills
- Outlook for the future.

Now write something in each category and an overall summary. In this exercise you are depersonalising yourself to try to get a more honest opinion of yourself by yourself. Ask the closest person to you to give you a score and compare the answers. Use this to link into the SWOT analysis discussed previously.

How to deal with reality

There will be many points in your later life when reality will crowd in on your freedom of choice. Apart from the moment of retirement itself, there will inevitably be major life events that will influence your freedom of action. Personal illness is an obvious one; less obvious may be the illness or disability of others in your life – most likely your partner but increasingly also your own elderly parents' requirements for care, supervision and support. Faced with such problems just when you were looking forward to greater freedom, it is understandable to feel resentful. You may feel life is cheating on you; that, as it were, you have paid your dues for many decades and life has failed to cough up the benefits.

These problems are unlikely to be as restrictive in practice as they may seem in theory. While it is true that they will place limitations on you, society in the West is advanced enough to make those limitations often bearable through medication, respite admissions and care homes. Your biggest problem is likely to be how to reconcile feelings of guilt with your desire to run your life as you wish. This is so important that I devote the whole of Chapter 11 to it.

When facing such difficulties, try the following five-part analysis.

(1) What is the basic problem?

With elderly parents, for example, the problem may not be so much a matter of your being 'on call' but the need to arrange specific services such as meals, medication or shopping.

(2) Is it permanent or temporary?

The direst problems can be endured with help if you know them to be temporary. Then you can set yourself little time goals – another week passed, or just another month to endure. It is the permanent problems that will force you to think very carefully indeed about how to cope, but it is pointless and exhausting to spend heavy-duty planning on temporary problems, for example, a painful hip while awaiting surgery as opposed to a permanent stroke.

(3) Can it be relieved or must it be endured?

'Learn to live with it' can sound such a heartless, even dismissive, phrase, but you do yourself no favours by clinging on to the hope of improvement where none is likely. This applies to your health, your financial or housing situation, social isolation or whatever other insoluble problem may arise. As a resourceful human being, learning to live with something means adapting your life around limitations in a constructive way; the longer you spend unrealistically expecting the situation to change, the less you will try to move forward in your life.

This could sound glib advice, easy to say when not faced with a problem, and no one denies the difficulties of putting such a strategy into practice. Yet you can probably think of people who have turned inwards on their problems, making them the focus of their life to such a degree that they exclude any personal growth or enjoyment. Eventually you lose patience with their complaints, which seem to become an end in themselves.

You can think of other people who are cheerful despite illness and yet others who are miserable despite wealth. This is not to say that illness is preferable to health or poverty to affluence; that would be nonsense. But just about any human situation is open to reinterpretation in a more positive way, a way that enhances your self-esteem rather than a way that demeans you into the role of being no more than a victim of misfortune.

(4) What help is available?

Now is not the time to be shy about asking for help; you have probably spent a lifetime helping others and trying to avoid being a burden. As far as possible you will want to continue that way, but this should not blind you to all the sources of help available. Some examples are advice on budgeting, social support, self-help groups, housing needs, benefits and carers groups.

(5) How important a restriction is this on my freedom?

Try to be honest about this; does a problem demand all your attention or can you see ways of coping with it? Talk about such matters with others, who may have suggestions about coping that you had not imagined, because you are too close to the problem.

Overall, time nearly always helps; a problem that seems initially daunting will usually take on a more manageable appearance over a few days or weeks.

Your personality will influence how much help you need in coping with life's difficulties. You may be someone who has always avoided problems, a worrier, or someone who looks for practical solutions. These aspects of your personality will not change with age, except that age often brings an understanding that problems will sort themselves out and that it is not always the wisest thing to rush to solve a problem as soon as it appears.

Later life gives you the luxury of thinking a problem through in a way that time pressures made impossible earlier. Make use of that time to avoid the breathless panic to just do something, which at other times was the best response you could give to a worrying situation.

Case study

Within a few years of retiring Peter and Jenny enjoyed a comfortable, fulfilling lifestyle. All that was threatened when their son's marriage broke down and he was expecting to live with them again. At the same time Jenny's mother broke her hip, making her housebound and Jenny herself developed angina and was awaiting tests. Suddenly their ordered life was crumbling before them.

It seemed a set of insurmountable problems, with conflicting demands, new restrictions on their freedom and uncertainty about the future.

For a few weeks they found it impossible to make decisions and had to deal with life on a day to day basis, hurrying to Jenny's mother's house when called, trying to keep up moderate exercise and trying to support their son without alienating his own wife and children.

They decided to call a family conference to discuss their worries and look at strategies. They wrote down a brief summary of each problem as indicated earlier and found that the real issues were clearer than had at first appeared. Jenny's mother's problems were going to be permanent; they put that to her and discussed their own situation frankly. Their son's problems, though devastating, they felt would be temporary.

In a moment of insight, they realised that it made more sense for their son to move into his grandmother's home, where he would enjoy more freedom and could act as a carer and co-ordinate her care package. Both would benefit from this arrangement and in fact draw satisfaction from being mutually supportive without the frictions of a parent–child relationship.

This gave Jenny the space to think of her own health problems; she found that she experienced less angina once her son had moved out but still decided that she needed to go on to heart surgery. It helped her greatly to reduce her anxieties to make plans for holidays after the surgery and to look forward once again to a happier life.

The most effective way to cope with change is to help create it.

L. W. Lynett

3

How to Plan Ahead

In preparing for battle I have always found that plans are useless, but planning is indispensable.

Dwight D. Eisenhower

Case study

Jim and Mary were in their 60s and had been retired for a number of years. Financially they had no problems and appeared quite content in their regular routines. Inwardly things were rather different. The initial euphoria at finishing work lasted for a few months until it became just a fact of life that they were no longer held to work routines. But somehow retirement was not what they imagined and as each year passed this feeling grew stronger. Although they were no longer constrained by work and outside pressures, their lives seemed as busy, but in a more random way. Emergencies still happened, there still seemed to be no time to do the things they really wanted. They felt as if time was slipping through their fingers. They had both had plans about what they would do but those too somehow failed to materialise, crowded out by the events of the day. Yet when they talked things over they had no difficulty in deciding what it was they really wanted to be doing.

The surprising thing was that they had both had demanding jobs with busy agendas that required them to balance multiple demands.

They knew they needed to plan, yet felt that the very act of planning went against the spirit of the third age they were in. It was meeting an old work colleague that altered their perception. He had never struck them as being particularly organised, yet it emerged that he had sat down soon after retiring and worked out a plan. They looked at it. It was a simple thing, with quite a lot of crossings out, but they could see how it gave a structure to his life. It was with a certain feeling of indignant pride that they decided that this was something they had to do themselves before they were entirely overcome by day to day living.

Start now!

The rest of your life is not a boat you can miss! The rest of your life does not begin the week after next, the day after next, even the next hour. Like a boat cutting through real water, your life consists of a path through real time. The curve of the water at the bow is here and now; the water just a mere fraction ahead is the future. Therefore your life path is constantly at a junction of the now, the past and the future. At any and every moment you have the opportunity to say 'I will do this and not that. I can choose to take this path and not another.' So the opportunity to start planning for your future health and happiness is not a single point that you must liaise with, a single moment which, once missed, is lost. On the contrary, you are constantly being given the chance to make decisions about your future and you need never say to yourself that you have left it too late.

This is a great freedom. Relax a bit; no one is holding you to a schedule, no one is setting you a deadline. But don't relax into total indolence, because there are decisions to be made and plans to be set. So, in the knowledge that you can never be too late, why not start a little earlier than you might have thought?

The very fact that you are reading this book implies that you have begun to think ahead. Do you feel awkward about this? Perhaps people have said to you 'If you start thinking about later life, you'll think yourself into old age.' What nonsense. If you dream about a holiday in India, do you wake up on the Himalayas? The idea that thinking about old age will interfere with your current life is incorrect. But you can see a grain of truth in the warnings. It's not right to become obsessed or over-concerned about things 5 or 10 years hence, at the expense of devoting attention to your current life. It all calls for a sense of proportion. If you find you are getting obsessed about the future, you probably have unconscious worries about your future which you need to confront. Or there may be serious deficiencies in your current life that you need to deal with.

In a sense, if thought of the future raises in you not a quiver of apprehension, delight or anticipation, there may also be a problem. A quiet mind, in these circumstances, may be more a reflection of complacency than of wisdom.

So start now. Just once in a while look ahead, think of your future not as a passive event that will overwhelm you but as a more plastic situation that you can influence. To return to our boat, with forewarning you can influence the speed and direction of the boat, even though you cannot influence the weather or the state of the water. But also at any given moment it is much harder to make instant adjustments to the boat, whereas just a little anticipation gives you far better control over where it is going. Similarly with planning your future; a few simple adjustments now can set your course more easily than frantic adjustments as events crowd in. Of course you cannot influence life's weather – the fortunes or misfortunes and the squalls; but it is far easier to set a reasonable overall course than to cope with last-minute turbulence.

The opportunities in retirement – work, choice, freedom

Whatever your personal aspirations, you should give thought to the following: your work options, the choices you have and the freedoms you enjoy.

Work

There is no biological reason to give up work at a particular age; it is only relatively recently that people have even had the luxury of stopping employment. No laws say that you have to devote yourself to a life of idleness. On the other hand, most jobs and professions do specify a retiring age, so to that extent the matter is taken out of your hands, at least as far as full-time employment goes. But increasingly, companies wish to retain their older workers' expertise. Or you may have a hobby or profession that you can continue after an official retirement age. Your decision will be influenced by financial needs, the pressures of the jobs and the requirements of others.

Choice

You may feel that your choices are limited as you get older. This may be more a problem of perception than of reality, except where there are sheer physical demands on you which you can no longer fulfil, for example in the building trade or as a result of illness.

It is important to realise that your choices are in some ways more open than during your working life because certain basic requirements have become less pressing: things such as the need to actually earn a living, the lack of necessity to seek promotion or to maintain your position within a company. You may feel quite happy that you have achieved what you wanted in life and that you can accept a lower status job or income level, secure in your own sense of self-esteem and having attained what you want by way of material things.

Freedom

Freedom after many years of work can paradoxically seem a burden in itself; now it is down to you to fill what can seem a surprisingly long day. This is a theme we keep returning to, because it is such a fundamental aspect of your life post-retirement, yet one that can become invisible, like the air we breathe. You need to keep reminding yourself of your freedom and the paradox is that the best way of doing this is by setting limits on it. To really appreciate freedom, you must have some restrictions. These are self-selected and should be as pleasurable as possible in themselves, yet it is by contrast with these that you can keep alive enjoyment of your freedom, just as fresh air is more pleasurable when you emerge from a musty room.

Constraints on opportunities (family, health, income, commitments, etc.)

As part of your self-assessment it is helpful to decide how much of what you did (or failed to do) is through the influence of others and how much is down to yourself. This will help you to see how the way ahead is likely to go. Perhaps previous obstructions to a fuller life have ended – the lack of time or the unsatisfactory relationship that left you with no mental energy for going forward. Perhaps you dedicated your life to your family and others to a degree which hindered your own development and which you now regret.

This is a complex situation because you may derive considerable pride from seeing how the objects of your devotion have fared or how relationships have endured despite difficulties. These immensely important (and unrepeatable) experiences should counterbalance any regrets about how your life has gone and can almost certainly be interpreted as achievements rather than lost opportunities.

Health issues may also have influenced your way through life and could also engender bitter thoughts. These too could be turned around and seen as obstacles about which you have to think creatively to overcome them or to else live within their constraints of, say, a painful hip, angina, or chronic bronchitis. It is only right to be realistic about how such constraints might influence the coming years. Clearly you are not going to overthrow the restrictions of heart disease as a result of hitting 60.

How to discover goals and worries

Write down the things you worry most about, random words about the future, key phrases and your reactions to them. Keep a list handy; as things occur to you just jot them down. The things that come to mind first are the obvious ones, health concerns, income, etc. That these come to mind first does not mean they are unimportant; on the contrary. But the things which emerge later may be the more awkward matters to deal with, as they tend to come from that subconscious attic where we chuck those awkward emotions we think we may have a use for one day but cannot bring ourselves to deal with immediately.

Eventually you should be able to group your concerns into a few categories. Likely ones are money, health, relationships and hobbies. Less obvious ones may be socialising, religion, boredom, fears for example of ageing, responsibilities to others.

You will probably end up with something like this:

Money: Savings, income, insurance, inheritance issues.

Health: Current health problems and their prognosis. Current symptoms which may foreshadow future health problems; goals for fitness and activity; health insurance.

Relationships: Health and financial relationship with partner, children, parents.

Hobbies: Current interests; whether feasible in older age; interests that appeal.

Socialising: Are you a people person or do you prefer your own company? This will have implications for how you spend your later life. Are you easygoing or do you have a reputation as being awkward? Do you want to make new friends or are you quite content with your existing ones? Is there a difference between yourself and your spouse/partner in this?

Religion: Is this an important part in your life or do you see it becoming one? For comfort reasons or as a means of socialising and social support?

Boredom: Does older age fill you with apprehension? Are you so tied up in your current jobs, roles and responsibilities that you find the prospect of years without them daunting, worrying, scaring?

Fear of ageing: This is a deep fear for many. In your case, why? Do you foresee decay, loss of power, loss of physical function, loss of freedom?

Now you should have a framework for dealing with apparent

difficulties and making sense of the array of concerns and choices that await you.

Goal setting, change and adaptation

There are some principles about planning which should be understood. Number one is that it is not essential; not everyone feels that life needs a plan. If that is the case, read no further. However, most of us do welcome the order and organisation that planning allows. For these read on, while understanding that a plan is an aid and not a straitjacket.

Here are some fundamental steps in the planning process. We go into each of these in more detail.

- You have to set goals
- Goals must be realistic
- Have a way of judging how you are doing
- Set yourself some challenges
- Use reliable information
- Co-ordinate your plans with others
- Be flexible
- Agree review periods and the criteria you will use.

You have to set goals

You have to identify what you want to achieve and when. We hope our planning tools will help you identify these goals for yourself, or else simply use your own categories. The importance of having a goal is that you know what you are aiming at; this focuses your activity and should make it more economical in the sense that you do not get distracted into false goals, wasting time, effort, money and emotional investment.

In deciding on goals, it may be helpful to refer again to the SWOT analysis (see page 21).

Goals must be realistic

There is nothing worse than dreaming up totally unattainable goals, realising you will not achieve them and then reproaching yourself for failure. This is an empty exercise. The idea is to agree things that are reasonably achievable. Yes, you may have to make an effort to achieve them (I hope you do); yes, you may find the thought of change in order to hit a goal uncomfortable. But as long as the goal is realistic, you will experience true satisfaction in hitting it.

If in doubt, here are ways of deciding if a goal is realistic.

- Do you feel comfortable thinking about it?
- Have you achieved anything similar before?
- Do you feel embarrassed discussing it with others?
- Would you feel upset if you failed to achieve it?
- Are there others you compare yourself with who have achieved similar goals?

It may be helpful to rank your goals and the difficulties of achieving them. Here is one way: what is required in terms of:

- Physical effort
- Mental effort
- Time
- Money?

Goals may be safe, achievable, enjoyable. Goals demanding a lot of time and effort may simply be too much. Think about your reasons for selecting such goals carefully. On the other hand, easy-to-attain goals may not be worth achieving or may not merit being called a goal, perhaps being simply an adjustment to your lifestyle such as walking more.

Have a way of judging how you are doing

This may involve certain sub-targets, such as achieving a certain level of fitness, dealing with certain health problems, researching new hobbies, getting to know the grandchildren better. The beauty of breaking major goals down into sub-goals is that you can congratulate yourself as you go and not pin all your hopes on hitting one big target. For most individuals this fits better with human psychology, which responds better to frequent rewards than to one possibly distant and ill-defined goal. To reinforce this, think of the reaction that talking about a pension plan gets from a 20 year old.

Set yourself some challenges

This is not to lose sight of goals being realistic, but it can be too easy to go for more of what is familiar. If you are comfortable with this, fine. Yet consider how rewarding it could be for you to make this period of your life one when you achieve some dreams. At a time when it is easy to loose self-esteem and status, here is a method of ensuring that you keep up performance in your own eyes as well as in the eyes of outsiders. Go back to the section above on setting realistic goals. Perhaps you can think of one or two which are demanding and which do seem to call for an unusual investment of physical or mental resources. Could these be ones where the satisfaction of achieving them would more than repay the effort called for?

Use reliable information

Now is not the time to guess how things can go. You want to get decent information about the goals you are setting and the background you require to judge their suitability. Use libraries, consult colleagues, the Internet, organisations for older people, trade associations, public organisations like the BBC. There's plenty of information out there so there should be no excuse for misinterpreting your future.

In a similar vein, try to make your assessment of yourself realistic. Put more weight on what you did achieve rather than on what you hoped to achieve, on concrete results rather than good ideas that came to nothing. Again, do not underestimate the advantages of your new situation, bearing in mind that lack of time or opportunity may explain why goals were not achieved earlier.

Co-ordinate your plans with others

Who are the significant others in your life? What are their plans, and how do they impinge on your own? Do they set limits on what you can do (for example, sick partners), or is it more a matter of a bit of intermeshing and of agreeing mutually acceptable aims?

Be flexible

Goals that are apparently important and valuable at one stage may come to appear valueless in the light of events. Goals that you might set just before retirement you will want to revise after a few years, and after a few years again, as your abilities and interests vary. This is good; you do not want to get into an era of unchange and unthinking routine. You should be setting yourself new targets as long as you can.

A useful test is to ask these questions of any goal:

- If I miss this will I feel upset, irritated or relieved?
- Is this goal central to other plans?
- Am I doing this for myself or for others?
- Is this goal in any other way still important to me?

In the light of this you may wish to review the goal. Perhaps you are asking too much of yourself. If so, redefine the target or drop it altogether. Or have you lowered your expectations of what you can achieve? Ask yourself again how important the target is to you and question yourself again as to the resources you feel prepared to put into it, remembering that ultimately this is for yourself and not for another.

Agree review periods and the criteria you will use

It may be once a year, it may be more frequently but you should have some plan for keeping a check on how you are doing. Certain items will demand regular review – your finances, perhaps, or your accommodation. Others need just a periodic review of whether you are on target or not, for example in terms of new interests or in terms of improving your health. If you set realistic targets to start with, these review periods should emerge pretty well logically from your framework.

At a review you need to ask:

- What progress have I made against the criteria I set?
- What remains to be done and can I do it?

- Have my feelings changed about this goal (see above)?
- Do I need to alter the target, the time scale or the criteria?
- If I abandon or downgrade this goal, how will I feel?

Role models

I talked earlier about some healthy daydreaming. It is unlikely that your imagination will rush to extremes, because maturity will not let it. But equally, your imagination may well be constrained by the way you have led your life up to now, so you may have already ruled out on non-rational grounds opportunities that you should explore. This is where a role model can be helpful. This is not such a bizarre concept. At all ages people have mentors, guides, gurus, if you like. These are people who will discuss things with you, mull over decisions, and make suggestions. They may have been successful in the field you are considering; or perhaps not so successful personally but they know how it is done, in the same way that rocket scientists can design a rocket though they may never be fit enough to travel in one. In these ways a role model can help focus your planning, open your horizons, reassure you that things are achievable.

You may wish to jump straight to the Charlton Hestons of this world, the John Glenns, the Queen Mother. Why not read some biographies about such people? You will see that things were far more complicated in their lives than might appear from their public image only. Focus on certain things. What were their talents? How did they use them? What role did luck, chance and fortune play? How did they cope with setbacks? What did they regret about their lives and what did they most enjoy? How did they cope with changes in fame, fortune, health? How did they look after themselves? What are their 'secrets' for a long and happy life?

As well as choosing people who have lived long lives and remained successful and vigorous, choose others who have had long lives but have been dogged by problems. How did they cope with these, what pulled them through?

Famous is fine but can seem unrealistic (though we have more to say about this below). So now think of role models among friends, colleagues, acquaintances. What do you admire about them? What makes them stand out from the thousands of people you have met in your life, so that they seem particularly appealing to you? Be honest; is it a matter of envy, pride, and jealousy? If so, about what exactly? Are they happy, are they fulfilled, could you imagine yourself following their path in life?

Now put yourself into their shoes. Imagine being this person. You are Hillary Clinton or Margaret Thatcher. Imagine following her life. How would you have reacted at major life events? Would you have acted as she did or would you have had a whole insight of your own? In fact, could you have coped with some of the problems they had?

And what about the happiness? How does their happiness strike you? Are the sources of their happiness things that you can understand or were their priorities not yours?

You can see how what at first glance appears a childish strategy turns out to be a tool for your own self-evaluation and self-knowledge. Your flights of fancy about how good life has been for someone else get tempered by the reality of how life has really gone for them.

There is unlikely to be one single role model for you; you may admire one person for their social skills, another for professional skills, another for surviving against the odds, another for their looks, another for their confidence. Whatever. Write them all down and try to abstract some common features from your list.

And an anti-role model

While you are about things, think about some people who embody just what you do not wish to become. Again these can be drawn from both public figures and acquaintances. Think of those who perhaps had promise but never quite fulfilled it, or who achieved much but let things slide. Did they have health problems they neglected, personal problems that got out of hand? Can you identify things you would have handled more constructively and which you feel you could have overcome? And what of their effect on others? What are your own feelings in thinking of these people? What is it about their personality, lifestyle or appearance that irritates or repulses you? Can you see yourself in them and is this the way you are happy to go?

Having such a concrete anti-model may be an even more powerful incentive to taking care of yourself than a successful role model; we often learn more from other's mistakes than we do from their successes. The closer these people are to your own lifestyle or circumstances the more powerful the effect.

Again, write down the conclusions you draw from thinking about these people. For example,

- Were they lucky or focused?
- How did they cope with uncertainty and fate?
- Did they relax, and how?
- Was there collateral damage (family, marriages)?
- Were they happy?

Now you are armed with some tools. You know where you are going and why. You know others who have gone along that path and found contentment. You know others who have neglected themselves or who have just survived against the odds. You have some idea of where you are going in life over a reasonable time-span, and these plans take into account your responsibilities towards others and the plans that others have for themselves.

A goal of the year

This may seem a strange concept, one that you can do without in later life. Why set yourself any sort of target, let alone an annual major one? No longer are you the head of sales, motivated to hit a quota, or a clerk called in for a regular check on your work by a half-smiling personnel officer. Or were you perhaps that very employer or personnel officer, dutifully fulfilling your employee reviews whilst harbouring some guilty feelings at holding their life in your hands?

The idea of an annual goal, strange as it may seem at first thought, is to encourage and to maintain your personal growth and with it your mental vigour. A major goal each year will be a focus to review, challenge and change some aspect of your life for the better. The alternative – relentless routine – is comforting but unfruitful. This is not to deny the value of routine, which we recommend elsewhere in this book. Rather, it is to make routine your ally for development instead of a comfortable excuse for complacency.

Think of it as process of annual review much as a company might review its performance regularly and produce a 'state of the company' message. You can review your year's achievements, the difficulties as well as the successes, and consider how things could be improved for your greater comfort, happiness, security or mental stability.

Here are some areas you might consider:

Comfort: Housing, cost of living, cost of utilities, major repairs and redecoration.

Happiness: Relationships with others that are causing problems, hobbies, social activities, and relationships with families or friends that may have lapsed.

Security: Personal safety by way of secure housing or transport, practicalities such as good footwear, supports when walking, financial security.

Mental stability: This could include anything threatening your peace of mind – health matters, a sense of deterioration either personal or in loved ones, failures in the last year that you could learn from or failures in your past life with which you have yet to be reconciled.

Having identified your goal (or goals), consider what needs to be done. Your choices will be to:

• Reconcile yourself to something that cannot or should not be changed
• Plan for change
• Set a target by which you will know when you have been successful
• Reward yourself – though much of the reward will come from achieving what you had set out to do.

As part of this process there will be a confrontation with difficulties you can do nothing or little about. This will call for a mental accommodation. With other things you may be able to achieve much less than you set out to do. Here there need be no sense of failure, but try to congratulate yourself on what you have done rather than to reproach yourself on what you have left undone.

Do you need all this?

Strictly speaking, no. It could be that you view any personal growth you achieve through this strategy as trivial at best or at worst not worth the mental effort. On the other hand, without this strategy, or perhaps some diluted form of it, you may find yourself vaguely dissatisfied with your circumstances without quite being able to identify the source of the dissatisfaction. This is not to suggest that all of later life can or should be a period of undiluted happiness and peace of mind – we know this is not the case. What I am suggesting is that you take the initiative in coping with this stage in your life, otherwise you may be sure that plenty of other events or outside influences will take the initiative from you.

Case study

It was with considerable embarrassment that Bob and Helen called their annual general meeting. They decided that sending out formal notices was pretentious but they did set up a board marked 'Agenda items' on the fridge, on which they encouraged each other to note areas of concern. For a few days nothing appeared more serious than 'eat more fruit' or 'get carpet cleaned'. One morning, however, Bob was surprised to read: '?Voluntary work with teenagers???' He said nothing but resolved to think more seriously himself. So it was that Helen in her turn was surprised to read 'Do we need two cars?'

Now that there were no holds barred, the more demanding items emerged: take up bridge, see grandchildren more regularly, have my wardrobe colour co-ordinated. At the point that the board was overcrowded, they called an interim AGM (half a bottle of wine and a glass of mineral water each) and tried to edit the board back to more manageable proportions. They graded the various suggestions 1 to 5, from 'interesting but not essential (1)' to 'yes, immediate action (5)'. In this way they identified areas that really did warrant discussion and areas that just needed a minor change in their routine

– such as eating more fruit (to which Helen added 'and walk to the fruit shop to buy it').

The formal AGM was a splendid affair (a bottle of wine job) but beneath the ceremony they were careful to try to put into words their feelings about each item as precisely as possible. To defuse the embarrassment they produced short written notes about the more demanding items such as giving up one car – which they found formalised their thoughts and helped to crystallise the issues. For example, giving up one car had repercussions financially and about increased exercise and reliance on co-operation for going out, and it raised questions about whether to change the other car and if so whether to buy something to keep for many years, etc., etc.

Taking up a new hobby raised questions about dissatisfactions in their life with existing arrangements and why. A discussion about aspirations led to an acknowledgement about clashes between some of their aims and some of their ways of relating to other people, for example one enjoying more solitude, the other feeling more of a need to meet people.

They ended up with several wineglasses needing washing and a series of resolutions put into as definite terms as they could manage by that stage in the proceedings. By the light of next morning they felt they could abandon a couple of resolutions which looked more heroic by daylight than they had by moonglow, but that left a core of five items that they felt represented a significant programme of change for the coming year. Of those they nominated one major goal – to give up one car- and decided how to reward themselves: by a week away at a particularly favourite part of the country, paid for simply from the savings from insurance and road tax alone.

They decided to leave the agenda board up, and found that suggestions appeared quite naturally as the year proceeded.

A man must make his opportunity, as oft as find it.

Bacon

Questions and answers

Q: I feel quite happy in my life. Why bother to change? A: You are in a lucky minority. Keep happy, but keep a note of your aspirations in life.

Q: I'm keen to develop but my partner is reluctant: A: As long as there is no tension between you, discuss your plans frankly but be prepared to compromise. If this shows up significant tensions you may need to discuss more formally how you both see the way ahead.

Q: I'm not prepared to rock the boat in order to achieve some goal I never knew I had. Can't we just leave well alone? A: Of course.

Q: My role model just got busted for drugs. What do I do? A: Think what you would have done in his/her circumstances.

Q: All the things I can think of doing are short term: A: You may well have organised your life not to worry about longer-term goals. Relax, but be aware of changing aspirations.

Q: Thinking of changing makes me unhappy because I think my life was unfulfilled. What should I do? A: Painful as it may be, think over where life fell short of your aspirations. Writing it down makes it easier. Now see whether you can rectify any of those setbacks through other people or other activities. Talking to others who have been similarly disappointed may help. Think of role models who you know have faced the disappointments you did and overcame them.

Q: I'm in a hurry to get lots of things done. How can I decide on priorities? A: Use the simple priority system mentioned earlier. Then leave it for a few days and see whether you would alter the priorities. Discuss with family and friends and review again. By now a realistic order of priorities should have emerged.

4

How to Develop New Interests (and Why)

Somewhere, someone is looking for exactly what you have to offer.

Anon

Previous interests

Few people reaching retirement age do so without having some passions and occupations, unless you are one of those who have been too tied up in simply coping with life to do so. A fruitful way to discover new interests is to look at what has interested you in the past. The following is a useful and enlightening way to categorise those interests:

- Absorbing
- Amusing
- Intriguing
- Worthy

Let us look at each in turn.

Absorbing

These are passions you may have enjoyed for many years and it would be surprising if you had not already pursued one such passion to some extent. It is remarkable how people find the time in otherwise busy lives for such absorbing interests, reflecting the deep satisfaction they provide.

Your main absorption may have been your work or your family, in which case you do face a problem as you get older and leave those preoccupations behind.

One way to judge how important an interest is to you, is to ask yourself: 'How would I feel if I could no longer follow this pursuit?' Your reaction will tell you how hard you should try to continue in one form or another.

Work and family; work or family?

What happens if work proves to be your all-absorbing interest? This is a problem but one well worth identifying as early as possible in order to plan what to do to avoid a gap in your life after retirement. Ask yourself what it is about your work that fascinates you. Is it the sheer love of the time spent? The rewards of esteem, status, money? Or the comfort of routine, certainty, familiarity? These are important benefits and our purpose in identifying them is not to diminish their importance but it is rather to see how to take the best from them.

The fascination could be subtler, even uncomfortable to admit to yourself. Did you enjoy work because it kept you out of the house and away from other responsibilities or away from other people? Your spouse, for example? Your children? Walking the dog? Was your career in some way a shield and a prop against engaging with people in a more honest way – a kind of role playing? Again, this in no way disparages these motivations; quite the contrary. All of us adopt roles in life and find that these roles have spin-offs that give more subtle and possibly more questionable satisfactions than we might be prepared to admit openly.

Was it the sheer power that you enjoyed, the response of others, be they employees or grandchildren? Many people enjoy work because it provides such advantages, which are frequently in glaring, not to say comic, contrast to their life outside work. If this applies to you, again do not despair and do not reproach yourself. You would not have achieved the position you enjoyed without ability, even if deep down you know how much luck, chance and the odd stab in the back may have helped you along. The healthy attitude is to celebrate those strengths and to try to find an outlet for them in a way that will continue to give you satisfaction and which might also give some benefit to society and your closest companions and contribute to your own personal growth.

This may call for an uncomfortable reappraisal of how you came to find yourself where you are in life and this process may simply neither appeal nor apply to you. This does not matter; you are who you are and the sum of what you achieved and it is unrealistic (and unnecessary) to plan to alter a personality which has seen you very well thank you for 40 or 50 years. Still, this book is about happiness as well as health and so we suggest that your future happiness will to some degree depend on analysing the basis of the satisfaction you gained from your working status and achievements. Harking back to page 26, these absorbing pursuits are likely to be at Maslow's self-fulfillment level of need.

Amusing

These are likely to be interests that you have played with over the years, followed for a few months or found absorbing at one time for reasons now hard to explain. The pattern will reflect the ways in which you have changed physically, mentally and socially over the years. There will be sports you have dropped because you can no longer do them; friends you have grown away from. Or there may be things you now do without quite knowing why you continue to do so, which while away some evenings pleasantly enough but which you would not miss too much if you no longer did them.

The test here is to ask yourself again: how would I feel if I could no longer follow these pursuits? Chances are you will reply: I would miss this aspect or that aspect, the social side, the relaxation side. In other words these pursuits are answering nothing as deep within you as those absorbing pursuits reviewed earlier. They are true amusements: something that helps time go by and keeps you happy in company with others. Typical items are going rambling, meeting at the pub, going to the cinema, reading particular books.

Taken individually there is probably no one amusement you would miss desperately. Taken as a whole they will add up to a delicate infrastructure to your life, important to nurture. In other words the whole is more important than the component parts. Here is a clue as to how to go forward: change within stability. In other words, you can safely abandon or down play any of these aspects of your life, if you want, without jeopardising your happiness, as would be the case with abandoning the absorbing areas.

It is worth considering whether it is time to stop any of these pursuits or to reduce your exposure to them. If you are going to make such a change, do it while you have the energy and ability, or you risk being stuck with amusements because you didn't seek new ones when you could. And amusement can easily become boredom or irritation.

The range of amusements is bound to reduce as you get older and practicalities of health, mobility and concentration come into play. But that could be a very long way off.

Intriguing

Here is where your life could begin. Think of those activities you always promised yourself you would try. The ones that seem so fascinating to others, though you can't quite see why. It may be a game such as bowling or bridge, a charity that seemed too time-consuming to support but which others tell you they enjoy very much. Travel, cooking, computers, languages: the list is endless – so large in fact that it may seem bewildering to know where to begin.

It is worth keeping a note of what intrigues you, because you might forget them unless you act on the impulse. Talk to others; see what enthuses them and consider whether this would enthuse you too. What are the activities they say they just can't miss, that are such a laugh? That make their spouses say 'No good planning to meet that day, you'll never drag him/her away from X'? Can they explain the fascination? Can you try it out without commitment? Do you feel a bit silly to consider it? Is it right for you now? You won't know till you try and if others do it, why not you? How about things that intrigued you in your youth, or aspects of your career you thought you ought to explore if you had time, or reason? Now that it may have no practical value, it might, ironically, be just the time to look again.

Worthy

This would include voluntary and charitable work, visiting others, organising things for others. The active retired are often ideally suited to this type of interest: they have time and patience and understand the problems faced by their age group. The range of activities is large, from 'adopting' an individual to driving, organising, even running quite a major operation such as an advice centre. Things to consider are:

- What will I personally get out of this?
- Do I want the responsibility of others becoming dependent on me?
- Am I prepared to undergo some training?
- Am I prepared to be supervised and held to standards?

Worries might include:

- Can I be sure I will say no to increasing demands?
- How time consuming will it be?
- Will it involve personal costs?
- Am I emotionally strong enough?
- Do I like dealing with people or with things?

Rewards lie in:

- Personal service
- Filling in where society falls short
- New relationships
- Gaining new skills and expertise
- The satisfaction others derive from your skills.

Many older people find voluntary work or community service immensely rewarding; volunteers are usually in short supply, so you are assured of a welcome. You can use your existing expertise, personality and training to help others; for most people this is one of the most enjoyable ways of making use of their health and abilities.

- If you are considering something worthy, do not feel guilty at seeing what is in it for you.
- Where appropriate, put limits on your involvement and make these clear from the start.
- Identify a way out.
- If it gets to be a chore: think, reconsider, stop, leave!

Having thought about all this, the next step is to see whether you can take the best of these opportunities and incorporate them into your new life.

How to find new activities

Preliminaries

It can be a killer to apply deep planning to activities intended to amuse and develop you, but a little bit of planning can help you sort out possibilities from the mass of options.

Ask yourself these questions:

- How much time can I give?
- Can I afford it?
- Are there other resources I must commit, such as travel, days away, equipment?
- How will this slot in with my other commitments?
- What does my partner think?
- Can I do it?

'Can I do it' is deliberately last, because you are wise enough to know yourself. You are unlikely to take up bungee jumping in your 80s – though you might! However, if you do have some doubts, ask your friends, speak to people in the field, perhaps shadow them for a while.

Build on what you know

Everyone has expertise in something, though it can easily be over-looked. What you may regard as an unremarkable, almost uncon-scious skill, others may regard with amazement. It could be cookery, planning, gardening, map-reading. The things you are most likely to overlook are skills and interests linked with your previous work: you took them for granted through familiarity but they may strike outsiders as magical. How can you build on these existing interests and expertise in a way that gives satisfaction? This can be easier than striking out in some completely new area, where you are uncertain about your capabilities and staying power.

Finding new activities

Surely you don't need advice on this? But let us assume you have read this far because you do want to try something new and perhaps the analysis given earlier has not yet worked. You need a little help.

Begin with obvious sources of information; the local paper, the library, the local college and its list of evening or day classes. Look at the small ads in the newsagent or other local stores. Ask neigh-bours what they do. You will be amazed at the hidden network of activities within most communities. If you ever wondered what went on at home all day while you were at work, here's your answer! The local authority often co-ordinates the activities of local interest groups, so they are worth contacting too.

For many people religious organisations can be valuable for social as well as religious reasons. Even though you may not be observant, your local religious organisation can be useful as networking.

Being alone

Some older people may find themselves on their own through the disability or death of a spouse or partner, or because they are divorced or never married. Fortunately, there are organisations for singles, but it can still be a daunting prospect to go out on your own if you are not used to it. You may find it helpful to team up with others in similar circumstances who may themselves be on their own. Or many old friends who go out as a couple will be happy to include you in their social life, your own children may be too (but ask, don't assume!).

Being alone when trying new activities has advantages as well as disadvantages.

Disadvantages
- It takes courage
- You stand on your own performance
- There is no instant support and second opinion
- You have a fear of failure.

Advantages
- Be taken on your own terms, not as an appendage to someone else
- Enjoy freedom of choice and withdrawal
- Your mistakes are cheaper
- Be more spontaneous
- Be answerable to yourself.

How to cope with new experiences

It is understandable to be apprehensive about beginning new groups and activities. You may fear making a fool of yourself, or being rejected. These are not silly worries, any more than they were silly when you were trying to establish a social network in your youth. Older people are more set in their ways and outsiders are more likely to be resented than at younger ages, although, as a moment of thought shows, this is not unique to older groups.

It helps to:

- Get an introduction: someone who knows you and knows the group, who can introduce you around, arrange for you to meet the most appropriate people and ensure that people know what to expect of you as well as what you might expect from the group – because they will be a little apprehensive too.

- Go to a taster or beginner's session. The whole purpose of these is to welcome newcomers; the usual social barriers are lowered.

- Promote yourself. No one will know how good a snooker player you are or what a good organiser unless you tell them.

- Be sensitive to others – ask how you are doing, think before being too forward.

This may not come easily to you. 'I am who I am' you may say; 'Take me for what I am.' Fine, no one wants to detract from your self-worth and self-esteem. Nevertheless, you are seeking the benefits and will have to make some compromises if you really want to get in with the organisation. Once you are in, then is the time to exert influence, suggest changes and push rather more for what interests you. This is obvious really; this is the way groups work and how people influence others.

At the same time, they need you. Organisations need people; simple but true. And organisations for older people need you more than you might think; there is bound to be more of a turnover of members for obvious reasons. So bear that in mind, when being interviewed or introduced.

How to cope with being rejected

If you feel things are not working out, what can you do about it?

- Firstly, talk to whoever is in charge. Are they aware of a difficulty or are you being over-sensitive? Are there issues you can deal with? It can be as simple as that you are sitting in someone else's chair, or have taken someone else's place. Once you know what the problem is can you do anything about it? Do you want to do anything about it? Do you need the group enough to agree to a compromise? Or is what you are being asked not worth it in terms of what you are getting out of the group, in which case you may decide to leave.
- Put things in terms of what are you doing wrong: is there something you are not aware of? Much better to put things in this way

than to blame others for not fitting in with you, which leads to friction or else the exit door.

- Speak to other newcomers. How are they finding things, did they have difficulties and what did they do about it? Were they successful or have things not really changed?
- Is it the group or is it the subject?
- In other words, do you enjoy the new interest but not the people? Or does the interest leave you flat regardless of the other social benefits? Clearly, if the latter you have chosen wrongly and will just have to try again.

As a result of these approaches you should be able to decide whether to persevere or to call a halt and try elsewhere.

Having trouble finding your niche?

Go back to basics again. What exactly are you trying to achieve? Do you yourself want new social outlets or is this really what others tell you that you ought to have? Are you pursuing hang-gliding to satisfy some inner urge, or is it to keep up with a neighbour?

Things change

You can no more count on stability as you get older than you can at any other time of your life. The new interest which so intrigued you last year, may quickly pall, as may the new companions who seemed such good fun last summer. This is life and is not unique to old age, except that you may find the prospect of starting over again more daunting. This may lead you to compromise in ways you would not have done earlier in your life. You may worry so much about making a change that it inhibits you from confronting whatever you find unfulfilling in your current activities. There is no slick answer to this, because only you know how irritating things have got and the psychological (or other costs) of beginning afresh.

In this process it helps to remember that:

- Time is precious – don't waste it on the unfulfilling
- Change will get harder: if you are going to change, do it sooner rather than later
- Nothing is perfect, nor is it likely to get better as you get older
- Build on what you know.

What all this says is that it is better to do something about your dissatisfactions than to leave things to solidify. As you get older your time horizons become more limited; decision-making is more of a priority, not less.

Case study

Gillian was looking forward to a new cookery class at the local college, especially as it included group outings to sample different restaurants. Until the first lesson, she had not realised that the class had been running for three years, when it became obvious that most of the people there already knew each other from previous courses. They were supposed to work in pairs, but most people were already teamed up, leaving Gillian to work with someone she simply found incompatible. As the next meeting was little different, Gillian decided to have a word with the lecturer. Though the lecturer was sympathetic, she felt she could not intrude on other groups and hinted that Gillian was the one who needed to make adjustments. However, she did persuade the lecturer to hold an informal cookery tasting, giving people the chance to break the ice.

Unfortunately, the following week people went back to their earlier aloofness and Gillian felt as uncomfortable as ever. The major purpose of going was to make new friends, but this just wasn't happening. As a final effort, Gillian brought in a cake to celebrate her own birthday and this did stimulate some conversation, but again only briefly.

Gillian decided she could not invest any more emotional capital into such an unrewarding scheme, much as this went against her nature to give in. She had a word with the year tutor. She was more sympathetic and suggested Gillian might like to try a pottery class or something else where everyone was a beginner and consider a 'Cookery for Beginners' course next term, where many more people would be novices. It took considerable strength to give up and admit defeat with the first cookery class; her sense of relief was so great, however, that even though initially it was painful and even a little humiliating, she knew she had taken the right decision.

Developing new interests in later life

It's all very well to go out and get there in your 60s and 70s. But what about in your 80s? Or if infirmity limits your mobility; what then? Fortunately, in Britain there is a reasonable network of care and social support, though it may be harder to access this outside of cities and towns. This care extends into advanced old age, with transport facilities, day centres and clubs for the elderly. These may be run by the local authority, attached to hospital day centres and old-age homes, provided as facilities specifically for the elderly, or run by voluntary organisations.

Get information from your social services, library, church and other religious organisations. As you get older you will probably have more definite ideas on what you do and are more likely to prefer a fixed routine, with familiar faces. If possible, it is best if you can pre-plan your move from an active life to a more sedentary and settled one; it can be uncomfortable, and you are far less likely to take up new interests as you get very old.

Once again, this is saying that you have to work at the foundations for a happy and fulfilled old age well before you reach the stage of increased dependence on others.

Don't forget . . .

The Internet
Terrified by computers? Forget your fears. Here is a great new way to expand your horizons as you get older. You can contact people with similar interests, you might research your family history, search for long-lost relatives, research items from anywhere in the world. There are specialised resource sites for older people, such as http://www.iog.wayne.edu, or http://www.thirdage.com. Or you can just keep up with the news, read papers and magazines on all sorts of topics, listen to international radio channels, get medical information, choose films, shop. What is for sure is that by the time you are reading this section the information in it will already look old-fashioned, so quickly is the Internet changing.

What do you need? A computer and screen, a modem (phone line) and an Internet service provider. Joining a service provider is now generally free. But allow for the cost of the phone calls while you are on-line. Even so, this expense compares favourably with going out for a few drinks or coffee and the costs of travel. Later you might want to add a video camera. How can you learn about it? Start by sounding out your children and grandchildren or young friends. After they have got over their shock that you have even heard of the Internet, they will be pleased to initiate you into the not so scary procedures. Otherwise many colleges offer introductory classes for Internet users. It is easy.

And get yourself a comfortable chair.

Broadcasting – television and radio

Don't let familiarity dull you to the tremendous entertainment value of these old friends. With an enormous range of programmes, educational as well as entertaining, there should always be something to interest you, day and night. You might consider investing in a subscription TV channel in order to get access to an even wider range of viewing – the cost is much the same as travel to go out for entertainment.

Radio may not have appealed to you when you were younger and you may feel reluctant to try it now. Pity. There is an intimacy about radio that is comforting and cosy; close your eyes and imagine that the speaker, musician or actor is performing for you alone. Again, there is an enormous range of free radio. Why not experiment with some of the more unusual stations – the only investment is a twirl of your finger on the tuner. You may hear repeats of music you enjoyed and shows that entertained. Or you may find an insight into modern music and attitudes that is less shocking than you imagined.

Cinema and videos

These are relatively cheap entertainment and can be an ideal social activity. Invite others over to watch a video or to go to the cinema together. Why not take it in turns to choose what to watch? Others' interests may not be your interests, but experiment. The cost of videos is low and under your control; if you want a break for the toilet or popcorn, you can decide. Discover the wicked pleasures of going to the cinema in the afternoon, when the prices are often reduced.

Theatres and concerts

The theatre and concerts appeal to many people. These tend to be more expensive and may involve travel into a larger city though there are many excellent local choirs, orchestras and drama groups. With some research, you will find organisations that arrange trips at discounted prices and sort out the travel arrangements as well. Once again, going in the afternoon to matinee performances will save you money. Given that saving, you can afford to experiment, to see the shows that might not be your first choice but sound intriguing.

Case study

James had always regarded bingo as a complete waste of time, a major embarrassment and a totally frivolous way to spend his later years. For reasons incredibly obscure to him, two of his neighbours thought otherwise, even though in other regards they seemed perfectly normal, talked about politics and trimmed the lawn. Matters came to a head when they both turned down an invitation to have a drink in the garden because it clashed with some bingo event.

Seeing this as proof of their terminal mental decline, James challenged them to explain bingo's appeal. Their response (which his wife told him he should have expected) was to invite him to a session. This threw him into a depression, then worry as to what to wear. Were silly hats and smoking de rigueur? Assured otherwise, he agreed to go to a midweek session, though he insisted on parking some way away and wearing dark glasses.

Everything he saw only served to convince him how sensible his views were – the noise, the cheering, the frantic scoring, the silly caller. On the point of leaving, he gathered up his things, his brain only half registering the numbers. He suddenly realised he had come up bingo and experienced a rather embarrassing lift of spirits and even a half-hearted cheer. The evident pleasure of those around him at his win (all of £5) was curiously warming and reminded him of the time 30 years earlier when he had secured a contract to supply widgets at wodget prices that kept his factory going for three months. Surely that wasn't the last time he had experienced . . . elation? His friends wisely said nothing: they simply reset his bet and rearranged his things.

He had some explaining to do to his wife two hours later.

What James found, underneath the silliness, was companionship, a bit of routine, some excitement, some new faces, some stories to tell of near misses and modest wins. Rocket science it was not, but his neighbour the accountant was there too. Oh, but he always wore dark glasses.

Some myths about new interests

Older people learn less easily

There is little hard evidence of this, at least until you reach your late 70s. What is true is that your concentration wavers more easily, so you may have to learn in short sessions and revise old ground frequently.

Older people are resistant to change

Much change is fashion-driven and the older you get the more you recognise this and are likely to resist change for change's sake. So as a group older people are more conservative. See this as having balanced judgement rather than as a handicap.

There is no point

This is a counsel of despair that might be true only in extreme circumstances of illness and debility. Life begets life, apathy begets apathy. There is no sadder spectacle than someone who refuses to do anything for fear that death lies in wait and sees years later that he or she has wasted their old age. If you were once motivated but recently began to feel like this, you may have fallen into depression or other illness – it is worth seeing your doctor.

Be your age; it's undignified

Younger people often say this without insight into the process of ageing. Most older people feel they have a young mind inside an older body and would rather follow what their mind says than what their body suggests. There are limits; Bermuda shorts over cellulite is not a pretty sight and trying to keep up with ravers is just an embarrassment. Rely on your own sense of dignity and self-esteem rather than conform to someone else's idea of what people of your age should be doing.

Activity will wear you out

This is almost entirely false. Impact sports such as jogging will indeed make arthritic knees and hips worse, while sudden heavy physical exertion is hazardous at any age. That aside, it can only be of benefit to use your body and mind to the limits of their strength.

If you haven't developed interests by your age you never will . . .

There is a nugget of truth in this, though it overlooks how work may have squeezed out other interests. Earlier I looked at strategies for overcoming a barrier that is usually more psychological than real.

Recap

- Do you need new interests?
- Write down 5 reasons why and 5 why not
- Do you have contacts you could utilise?
- How would you feel if things did not work out?
- Given the choice, what do you most want to do?
- Given the choice, what activities do you most want to drop?
- Practicalities – cost, access, time, physical and mental ability

Possible pursuits

- Walking (this covers rambling groups, countryside walks, city walks; start by exploring your own town or village and its history; if you get expert enough you could even start leading such tours)
- Travel
- Writing

- Sports: bowling, tennis, badminton, swimming
- Computers
- Investing
- Local conservation and amenities
- Voluntary work
- Health, including your own.

Doing good to others is not a duty. It is a joy, for it increases your own health and happiness.

Zoroaster

5

The Skills of Maturity

The greatest thing in the world is to know how to be one's own.

Montaigne

Maturity and its benefits

We live in a youth-dominated culture – so says conventional wisdom. When you look at advertisements, what do you see? Youthful figures endlessly playing, smiling, doing, achieving. The models drape artlessly in exotic parts of the world or are thrusting aggressively in pursuit of some obscure goal which inevitably involves a mobile phone, a portable computer or long-lasting lipstick. To you, the music may seem unpleasant, the lifestyle ugly and selfish, the motivation sex or money. Where is there room for you in all this?

Elsewhere in the papers there are reports of companies de-layering, throwing out workers above a certain age and retiring others. Even prime ministers look younger and as for police officers . . .

Perhaps you yourself have been the victim of this culture; maybe you were retired when you felt you still had much to offer. Or do the attitudes of others leave you feeling undervalued, odd and worthless in a youth-dominated society?

It is a myth. You, older person, are the real power in society; it's just that advertisers don't like to admit it. Many of you are the ones with disposable income, wealth and time and all of you have an array of positive qualities that we will review in the rest of this chapter. Actually, advertisers and business do know this; they also know that you are not as swayed by advertising as the affluent youth market, so they direct their efforts there instead.

It is true that age does count in the workplace but this attitude is not as widespread as you might imagine. Look at professional firms and public companies. Certainly there are the high achievers in their 30s and early 40s and stories about high level bust-ups of people in their mid to late 40s. But take time to study those employees not in the immediate media spotlight. There you will see plenty of people in their 50s, 60s and even 70s still playing an active role and indeed still valued for some of the attributes we will consider.

Remember, too, that a youth culture is a particular feature of Western societies; attitudes are very different in the Far East and Asia. There, age is respected and even revered. While the adverts feature the same youthful role models, behind the scenes real power resides in the hands of the grey-haired and those societies are none the worse for it.

Quietly and efficiently, an older generation keeps society going behind the razzmatazz of the young. Not only at work and in the home, but also in an array of social supports and networks, it is older people who, through service, help and voluntary work, provide the essential infrastructure that makes a society a pleasant place to live in.

What are these strengths? Read on and prepare to blush – you never knew you were so great.

Wisdom

Perhaps this brings to mind a biblical or mythological figure, a white haired bearded prophet, a mysterious shrouded female figure passing on words full of obscure, vaguely troubling meaning. Not at all; your wisdom is a more down to earth affair and comes from having experience of life and of all the events which have contributed to it.

What does this mean? It includes all those social interactions over the years with friends, family and passing acquaintances. It includes the innumerable brief and forgotten interactions in shops, on buses and trains, in the street; all those half-forgotten parties, waits in airports and peering out at a scene waiting for the rain to clear; all those people into whose personalities you had a brief glimpse, whose life story was revealed for a moment in their tone of voice, choice of phrase, demeanour, thoughts, attitudes and memories.

Wisdom includes exposure to all life's uncertainties and problems. How to cope with them, the pleasurable as well as the more painful. The unexpected problems that you had to react to quickly. The more leisurely difficulties you had time to mull over and analyse. The difficulties that you never resolved and which have perhaps left some legacy of bitterness, sadness or embarrassment. All those excitements in life – they too posed challenges. Accepting the approval of others, perhaps knowing the gap between what you really achieved and what others think you achieved.

Then again there are all the worries and uncertainties you have experienced; in your youth you thought these were transitory but as you grew older you realised that they were an unavoidable aspect of a fulfilling life.

These experiences are the ones from which you gradually derived your wisdom. You may not think of it as wisdom; you may prefer to call it experience, know-how, or growing up. But just as you look at the flight of a bird with admiration, so others can look at you and see that what you regard as effortless looks remarkable to those who have yet to achieve your expertise.

What makes up this wisdom? There are as many philosophies of the old as there are elderly, but typical conclusions would include the following.

Everything passes

This means that sadnesses fade and happinesses do not endure. This does not make you morose, just cautious about extremes of emotion. You are more circumspect about emotional investment because you have seen it all before. To younger people you may come across as a little cold or unenthusiastic, and there is some truth in this. This may be why some companies want to get rid of older workers who seem to lack the required enthusiasm for every new idea, but at some point those same companies will also consult older, wiser and more mature heads who will ask the difficult questions – what if, what next, how, why and for how long?

Little is really new

Over your lifetime you will have heard so many grand schemes, fresh starts, great new ideas and sure-fire winners. There were successes, of course, otherwise society would not have moved forward over your lifetime. But for each success there have been so many failures and false starts. The old solutions keep turning up under new guises, the old emotional difficulties in new settings. The big change, at least during the twentieth century, has been in technology and it is technological change that has really driven so much innovation, from social structures to leisure, to work practices, to health, to financial instruments. People still strive to earn a living, to be happy and to be comfortable. Though the 'how' has altered, the 'what' is little changed.

This means that older people tend to look behind the hype and seek out the reality. 'How is this better?' they ask. 'What will this do for my family, society or myself?'

Others label this as, at best, caution, at worst cynicism that nothing is worthwhile. But you stick to your wisdom drawn from experience.

It's no good saying 'I told you so!'

People will accept your wisdom but they will not accept doom and sooth saying. Nor being wise after the event. These just irritate, because everyone can be wise after the event, and there is risk in every new venture. A better way is to say: 'I see your vision, but have you considered . . . ?' Or, 'In my experience (a) follows from (b). Have you allowed for that?' Or, 'That sounds great. I look forward to seeing the end result. And I hope you find room for . . .'

People and things are complex

Young people tend to regard others as one-dimensional – a great person, a walking disaster, a smooth operator, a whizz-kid. Later you may have been disappointed and become over-cautious, seeing the world as peopled with opportunists and tricksters, all in it for themselves. Eventually, you recognise and accept people's true complexity: at one and the same time they can be both honourable and untrustworthy, admirable in some respects and disappointing in others. You no longer base your judgement on only one aspect of their lifestyle or personality; rather, you are increasingly inclined to make allowances, to see things from their point of view with insight into their motivations.

This makes older people more tolerant than most young people. Again, this runs against the current mythology that age is resistant and youth is open-minded. In some respects this may be true, if your target is new music or a new colour scheme. But when it comes to interpersonal relations the elderly have the edge because they know the true range of behaviour possible for any one person.

You might object that this makes the elderly non-judgemental to the point of blandness and in some cases this is no doubt possible. Common experience shows that the elderly are just as likely to hold strong opinions about others, often deriving from things that happened many years earlier. But in fact the greater tolerance of the elderly makes them better people-persons, more sympathetic to others, better able to handle extreme emotions without letting things get out of proportion. Employers realise this and see the benefit of having older people deal with customer relations and complaints.

Seize the day

This famous injunction from Horace (*carpe diem*) is a natural wisdom for the elderly and not unknown to the young either. Take opportunities as they arise and deal with matters sooner rather than later. Life is what it is now; what is to come is uncertain. Beyond a sensible prudence about the future, avoid becoming preoccupied with what might be. Aim to deal with life as you find it and how it presents itself to you.

This philosophy has a natural appeal as you get older and offers empowerment rather than restriction. Unencumbered by work pressures, you are better placed to turn such a philosophy into action, more so in fact that when you were younger and had to temper enthusiasm with responsibilities

Most things can be solved

Your lifetime has shown the truth of this because problems that seemed insuperable at one time just crumbled away at another. Sometimes you were the one who thought it through and came up with the solution, at other times the solution came from others. At yet other times the problem just seemed to fade away, lose its significance or become resolved in dealing with some greater challenge or change of circumstance. You may have wondered whether to change your wardrobe for the latest jackets, then lo and behold, your old ones just came back into fashion.

Insight

You may not see yourself as having insight but almost certainly you do. Insight implies being aware of what is going on under the surface of events and experiences, seeing connections that are not immediately apparent.

Insight is understanding people's motivations without their having to spell it out to you. It can make sense of behaviour that otherwise appears inconsistent and irrational and the same goes for events. It is an ability to see the internal logic, which is not at all the surface logic. When a younger person says to you 'I see where you are coming from', they are really saying 'I have some insight into your position and your motivation.'

Insight is founded on experience of people, their behaviour and their explanations. Over the years without necessarily realising it, you have been building up a kind of internal rule-book of how things tick. A dictionary, if you like, that translates between the seen and the unseen. Here are some examples.

- A teenager says, 'Don't keep going on about studying.' This translates into 'I don't know what I want to do, but I can't admit that your ideas sound sensible.'
- A client says, 'Why didn't you advise me against making that decision', which translates into 'Something has altered that I can't tell you about, but I'm looking to blame you if I can.'

- Your spouse says 'We've had that couch rather a long time', which translates into 'First we'll build on a conservatory, then we'll redecorate, then we'll refurnish, and then we'll move house.'

The essential of insight is that you don't have to work at it too hard. It's very much an unconscious linking up, rather than a more conscious and painful process of analysis. It is a very high order of pattern recognition derived from years of seeing the gap between reality and illusion, and you built up this skill imperceptibly.

Some people do work at it, by pondering on what people have said and comparing that to earlier experiences and outcomes. Usually, however, insight is one of those things that just come as you get older; it can be a source of quiet satisfaction to yourself and appear an impressive psychological skill to others.

As with all human abilities, there is a range of skill; some people have an almost uncanny insight into things, others go through life blithely unaware of hidden motivations, goals and aims. Probably it cannot be taught. If you are lucky enough to have it, you will be valued for your opinion and help in resolving problems, adding to your general reputation as a wise person.

Patience and experience

Part of your wisdom is the wisdom of not having to rush; you know that things will happen whether you like them or not and that the chances of really critically influencing things are relatively slim. Those moments have to be judged with care and it is important to act on them. You are also more likely to identify them. This saves you a lot of wasted energy, worry, brain power and angst and is all part of the benefit of the learning process you have been following throughout your life.

The young will criticise this for not being proactive and not taking things seriously enough – perhaps of letting events overtake you. How far this is from the truth! Instead of reacting uncritically to every small change in your environment, your older brain is analysing the wider picture to select the moment when action is necessary. Some examples will show what I mean.

- The younger stockbroker might want to be in and out of the stock market and each blip of share prices is for him or her a signal to do something; whereas the older broker looks at the trend and takes a view on how the market is likely to move over the next few hours. Their results maybe the same, but the older broker's style requires much less energy.
- Another example from medicine. Junior doctors and medical students try to make sense of every symptom and to deal with it in isolation. They think, 'Ah, headache, what could that mean?' 'Oh, leg pains, how about that?' 'A fever, now what's going on?' An older, wiser doctor will see a total pattern of, say, infection, within which each individual symptom fits.

This cannot be taken too far; there comes a point when you see the pattern pretty well as effectively as you are ever likely to. You have peaked in a particular area, and you may think that thereafter things will deteriorate but this is not actually the case.

Tolerance

Tolerance in an older person – whoever heard of such a thing? Surely as you get older you become more intolerant, everyone knows that. Well, everyone is wrong. People confuse 'acceptance of the new' with 'tolerance'. It may well be true that as you get older you are more sceptical about the advantages of innovation; you have seen it all before, the hyped-up new broom which makes a lot of fuss and noise, only to achieve little more than the wooden thing it swept away. But that is not really to do with tolerance, which is more a question of accepting calmly all these so-called innovations. It extends to personality types, opinions, places, activities. As you get older you become more aware of diversity, of people's right to their own tastes and viewpoints in a way that the younger and less worldly-wise may find baffling.

Being your own person

One reason is that older people are more comfortable with who they themselves are. You are not a film star and never made big bucks or moved to that idyllic location or learned how to co-ordinate your bag with your shoes. This was once terribly important, for reasons which . . . somehow now escape you. Or maybe you do remember but the motivations have simply lost their power. You have reached a stage where you are tolerant of yourself. And if you can be so accepting of how you are, how much easier it is for you to be accepting of how others are too! After all, they have also had their aspirations, urges, accidents, successes and achievements and look where they are now. This is a very big bonus. If you are comfortable with yourself, you have the strength not to be made uncomfortable by others.

The uncertainty of youth

Contrast this with younger people, still finding their way in the world, still sculpting (and being sculpted) by life. The present is uncertain, let alone the future. They cannot rest satisfied with what they have achieved and where they are; that luxury lies years ahead. So, simmering in uncertainty about their own standing in life, they are impatient and intolerant of others. To acknowledge someone else's success carries an undertone of criticising your own achievements. Accepting the validity of someone else's viewpoint can jar with the strength of their own convictions.

It is easy to see how, for much of our early life, tolerance is a rarity rather than the norm. By later life you have nothing left to prove unless you choose to. This is not to forget what we have seen in earlier chapters: setting yourself new challenges can be a healthy thing; but these are challenges selected for their contribution to your personal growth, rather than targets set by an indifferent world.

Not complacent . . .

Is tolerance, therefore, just complacency? Or is it a negative 'I don't give a damn' rather than a positive response? Of course, it can be and often is − another reflection of not investing huge emotional efforts into little targets. But as you get older tolerance is a far more positive and valuable attribute, which helps life run a little more smoothly and amicably.

Not bland . . .

Nor does tolerance mean not having your own opinions, ideals or standards. On the contrary, as you get older certain attitudes are likely to harden and to become more deeply fixed. It is not just young people who make wars or start arguments; plenty of older people do become rigid in their views and intolerant of others. I am not suggesting that every older person is a guru, smiling benignly and dispensing good thoughts. What I am suggesting is that it is a strength typical of older people to be able to put things into perspective, distinguish between what is worthy of effort and what just does not merit a whole song and dance.

Tolerance as a tool

The tolerance of the old makes them natural mediators and peacemakers; they can present all points of view with due respect yet still focus on the greater goal. You may thus find a natural and congenial role dealing with family arguments or difficulties between your children and their own children, advising to your previous business or in dealing with people in a part-time job. You can be relied upon more to stay unruffled and calm while dealing with what needs to be done.

Patience

Patience with what you do and how you go about it affects so many things. At the most trivial level, it means not getting upset at waiting at a checkout for service. So you wait 30 seconds? Big deal. Patience is letting a car enter from a side road rather than claiming that 16 feet of road space for yourself. Do not allow others to make you feel guilty about taking your time. Settle yourself comfortably and then get on with the next task, rather than dash headlong forwards. Let younger people say, 'Get a move on' or roll their eyes in exasperation or make other even less subtle references to your slowness. Why shouldn't you not be patient and take your time, rather than run at the frenetic pace of the rest of the world?

These are minor examples. What about patience with a colleague whose work has deteriorated? Once you might have been tempted to confront the individual with a choice of getting better or getting out. Now you have the patience to wait for an explanation that you feel pretty certain will come. Or perhaps your own partner's slowness once infuriated you; you wanted to get on and get out about your business. As you get older, this frenetic dash comes to seem less necessary; you can enjoy the pace of the moment without feeling the need to cram in yet more activity.

Giving things space

In a way similar to tolerance, you can let events run at their own more natural rhythm, in the knowledge that things will happen whether you like them or not. Patience says that the world will go on regardless of your particular desires and in ways that you cannot always influence. It is a demotion of your own importance in the scheme of things, so that you accept that not everything has to fit in with your own schedule; there are plenty of valid reasons why your agenda can be secondary to that of someone or something else. What does this say about yourself?

Less self-importance

You value yourself as much as before but you do not over-exaggerate your worth. Just as you have a place in things, so things in turn have a place in other patterns that run to their own rhythms. You have learnt that always demanding to be first may have not only short-term benefits (you do get your can of beans 10 seconds quicker) but also longer-term disadvantages (others no longer seem to have time for you).

Patience is not passivity

This common misconception says that if you wait your turn or are not demanding, you must by definition be a passive victim of whatever life bowls you. I do not accept this. On the contrary, as you get older you should retain a strong sense of your own value and the validity of your point of view. Bad service remains bad service, unpunctuality does not get excused because someone is 75, nor should organisations disregard your requirements because your hair is greyer than that of the person making the decision. The patience we are considering flows from a true sense of perspective about priorities – when it is reasonable to demand action and when it is reasonable to let events unwind.

Inner calm, outer calm

Patience should be a reflection of general inner satisfaction with how things are. Letting life take its course is an expression of being happy with how you fit into life and its rhythms and an understanding that you cannot always usefully influence the rhythm of life; you no longer confuse noise and action with real progress.

Arguably this can be seen as meaning that you no longer feel as confident about influencing others and life as you may have done when you were younger. Some people may see this as a weakness, a deterioration in what you owe to yourself as you get older. I suggest a more positive angle, deriving from a surer knowledge of your own value and a greater insight into your place in the greater scheme of things. This might sound pompous, when all we are talking about is how quickly the waiter brings your coffee, but life reveals itself in the detail as much as in the grand set piece.

Memory and learning

It may come as a surprise to include these as strengths of the elderly, when the conventional wisdom is that these become more difficult as you get older. It is true in strictly biological terms that the power of memory declines as you get older; since memory is essential for learning, it follows that the ability to learn declines. However, that broad statement covers a far more complex situation which is widely misunderstood. For example, no one doubts that memory is greater in children as compared to adults, but we cannot move from that to saying that children learn more effectively than adults. Where does the difference lie?

Despite their greater learning capacity, children use their memory less effectively. This is because they lack the experience to make sense of what they are learning and without that experience know-ledge alone is of relatively little value. This is why older people remain effective in new situations even though, on strict tests of pure memory or learning capacity, there will be a decline from the late 30s onwards.

We shall go into this in more detail in the chapter on 'How to Keep an Active Mind' (page 153).

Pattern recognition

This wider ability is what you acquire as you get older and it destroys the myth about poor memory. As time has gone by you have, whether you were aware of it or not, become more familiar with events; at an unconscious level your mind has been making sense of the world for decades. Within your own career you will have been making sense of things in a more formal, less subconscious way by actually analy-sing problems and learning lessons from them. By maturity there will be ever fewer situations that are completely new; in most cases you can recall something similar, remember how you handled it and how it worked out.

This is a tremendous strength and more than compensates for changes in memory as time passes.

Task-specific learning

This is where there may be difficulties as you get older and where memory changes do make themselves felt. 'Task-specific' means learning purely factual information and being able to recall it. It is partly a function of short-term memory – the ability to retain facts for up to a few minutes – as compared to longer-term memory, where ideally you retain facts for ever for future use. In both of these there are declines as you get older and you may find this frustrating. You start to make lists, tie reminders around your fingers and resort to all sorts of other means of reminding yourself about things.

In an environment of rapid change this can indeed be a disad-vantage as you get older and this is the reason for the attitude about the declining capacity of the elderly. However, there are relatively few environments where this is crucial for the job, and the chances are that you will in time self-select yourself out of settings such as stock dealing, air traffic control and other jobs which demand a high level of short-term memory.

Experience compensates

All this is saying that you should not worry too much about declining memory as you get older – nor deceive yourself that it does not happen. You will discover plenty of strategies to deal with poor memory, from notes to personal organisers. Where you may need to use them will be in areas that raise no eyebrows and cause you no embarrassment. In most other areas of your life any memory changes will be more apparent to yourself than to others. Your trick will be not to expose yourself to environments where problems with your memory might prove awkward for you. Even then, others will make allowances for you; you might find this annoying or patronising but you can turn it to your advantage and enjoy the bit of leeway in your life that it offers you.

Experience will compensate, rather as background fills in a canvas; recognising the pattern means that new information can be easily slotted into a framework that you already carry in your head. This is so much more efficient than having to remember the whole framework – which is something you had to do, with pain and effort, at some stage in your life.

How to bring it all together

Now mix together all these skills of maturity – the wisdom and tolerance right through to the pattern recognition. Stir well and consider the outcome. What you have is an individual, different certainly from someone 20 years younger, but with qualities that more than compensate for the inevitable changes of age. While someone younger might be more mentally agile, you will benefit from a broader experience, from the insight that comes from having met problems, people, situations and attitudes in many different guises in many different settings.

Whereas someone younger might have to go through a brain-aching period of analysis and worry, feeling driven to perform by both internal and external agendas, you have the luxury of letting your unconscious mind do most of the work. You can compare the current situation with your lifetime experience. Working to a more leisurely agenda, and more open to ambiguity, the conclusions you come to will be at least as valid as those of a younger person and probably far wiser, more subtle and more psychologically sound than their decisions. You will avoid the pitfalls of rapid decision-making – coming to hasty conclusions on insufficiently weighed evidence and without taking into account the broader picture and the effects of decisions on others.

If this is what you wish to call wisdom, that's absolutely fine. One satisfying aspect of wisdom is that it is more in the eyes of the beholder than in your own eyes; to you it may just seem common sense. But sound common sense is not so common and not always sensible. Which is why the thoughtful older person can more readily acquire a reputation for sound, wise judgement that carries more weight than the slicker conclusions of younger people.

Does the world care?

It's all very well having this wisdom, but why should anyone care about it? How can it be to your advantage? Actually, plenty of organisations do care, having come to realise just how good older people are at dealing with more awkward aspects of a business – common examples are dealing with enquiries and customer complaints. Age is a positive advantage in certain selling positions such as pensions and financial advice, or in practising law and medicine. Certainly, clients want up-to-date advice, but what they also want is a feeling that the adviser can home in on their needs as an individual and sympathise with their situations, worries and aspirations. It can be difficult to define just what the feeling is, but people recognise it when it is there and reject false attempts to emulate it by others. They also understand that the facts are relatively easy to check and that it is more important to deal with someone who understands the question and where to find the facts if necessary.

Outside work, there are other contexts where these skills of maturity are valued. Within family settings it is often the older people who are called on to resolve family difficulties and misunderstanding. Wisdom, patience, insight and tolerance may be mocked at other times but they come into their own when trying to make peace within a family and perhaps helping others to cope with changing roles. Voluntary organisations too are ideal outlets for the skills of maturity, demonstrating that older voluntary workers can empathise in a way that younger people just cannot without appearing at best unconvincing and at worst patronising.

These are very major skills; they cannot be taught, they are acquired through that most personal and difficult of universities, life. Individuals will vary in how much they learn from life and the wisdom they acquire; as is so rightly said, there is no fool like an old fool, because by implication they have learnt nothing and lack the insight even to realise it. You probably cannot set out to acquire wisdom, as you might an academic qualification. Some people will never get it.

All the skills mentioned in this chapter can also become perverted in their effects. Witness the older person who refuses to believe that anything new is worthwhile, whose attitudes remain rooted in the experiences of years before, in whom tolerance become indifference and whose insight becomes cynicism about the motives of others. Their patience is a cover for the loss of their own self-esteem and their learning is confined to going over what is already familiar rather than risking exposure to the new and challenging.

Many older people become like this and it is through their example that others form the stereotype of the inflexible, judgemental, somewhat confused senior citizen. This is not necessary; if you recognise this and work to preserve the best, your old age can be the best time of your life for thoughtfulness and empathy.

Case study

Once, Pamela had been able to add up a column of figures virtually at a glance, never needed a shopping list and knew birthdays without consulting a diary. Latterly her memory had been letting her down and she forgot even her own daughter's birthday, while shopping trips involved a flurry of notes detailing what she needed. At the same time she had no difficulty in understanding the latest novels and comparing them with books read in the past. She felt acute embarrassment about her deteriorating memory and tried to pretend it was not happening, perversely 'forgetting' to take a diary or leaving her lists behind.

She came to question her worth and foresaw a steady decline into dependency and dementia.

Telling herself that this was the future, she was upset when her daughter's marriage ran into difficulties, and by the effects this had on her daughter's own teenage children. They all came to talk to her, initially with anger. Somehow she just knew that it was right to let each of them talk and not make any value judgements about what they were telling her. In time she came to see the whole family picture and the conflicts of expectations and emotions that were both the cause and effect of her daughter's marriage difficulties. This understanding came to her without effort and without her needing to analyse or mull over the emotions and attitudes she encountered. Eventually she felt able to offer explanations, other viewpoints and insights into how each individual's emotions were playing and interweaving with others in the family.

The marriage still broke up; her daughter and son-in-law still parted. But the atmosphere was changed from one of blame to one of understanding and regret, for which Pamela took the credit, being seen as a wise honest broker by everyone involved.

Discussing this with friends, she was surprised to learn that she already had a reputation for insight and that others had found talking to her helpful in coming to terms with their own problems. She learned of a vacancy at the local Citizen's Advice Bureau for a counsellor; aware she lacked qualifications, she applied in uncertainty. Three years later she continued to give support and a friendly ear to people plagued by money worries, family problems and work pressures. But she still had to write down the times or she was sure to forget to go.

6

You and Yours:
How to Maintain and
Nurture Relationships

*Age does not protect you from love but love to some extent protects you
from age.*

Jeanne Moreau

Spouses, partners, lovers and friends

Your journey into retirement and towards a healthy, content old age
is like that of a great cruise liner. Someone – preferably you – has set
the course, overseen the preparations, kept an eye on progress, looked
out for storms and had a darn good time. But that person – preferably
you – cannot do all this on their own; they rely on good relationships
with many other people, each of whom has their special role in
keeping the journey going. And these people will have their own
agendas, which you may not fully understand, and their own goals,
aspirations and difficulties. The attitudes of those people who are
relatively unimportant to you will not concern you much; the
attitudes of people you care greatly about will trouble you very much
indeed.

In order to maintain your emotional equilibrium during this great journey, you need to ensure some common agreement with those you care for about the general direction you are going in, and some degree of mutual agreement as to the value of the goals at which you personally are aiming. This does not mean that you must live your life for others; a degree of self-interest is entirely healthy. But if you live entirely for yourself, you will find conflict and emotional instability. Before analysing this further, here are some principles to bear in mind.

You deserve your own goals

It is not necessarily selfish to want the best for yourself, as long as you are aware of and allow for the feelings of others. Though the pursuit of personal happiness can be an entirely self-centred thing, most people's personal happiness relies greatly on the happiness of others. Therefore do not abandon your own goals for fear of what others may think. At your time of life your goals have a special significance that can only reinforce their importance for you. Gone are the times when you must subordinate your desires to the wishes of others; you have literally done your time and earned your freedom and that includes spending your energies in attaining those goals you feel most strongly about. It would be sad if it is only after retirement that you can strive for yourself, but in the real world this is often the case. So don't apologise for doing now what you've most wanted to do.

To jaw-jaw is always better than to war-war

The wisdom of this saying by Winston Churchill grows deeper as you get older. There are very few circumstances in someone's personal life that merit total aggression and a fight to the death and one of the strengths of growing older is in recognising this fact. Though younger or less mature people may threaten you with emotional blackmail, always strive to understand, sympathise and ultimately work something out rather than respond in their own terms of inflexibility or defiance. During your working life, war-war may have been the right strategy to achieve your career or professional aims. It is a disaster in interpersonal relationships, unless you want a later life in splendidly triumphant but lonely supremacy.

Compromise is not weakness

This follows from the previous. Compromise is not some peculiar weakness involving loss of face or capitulation; it is a normal arrangement to cope with what are so often otherwise mutually incompatible aspirations in our lives. We have all met people who are not prepared to compromise and seen what a miserable time they have of it. In the context of a career, their attitudes may get results, but, like aggressive behaviour, it can be a catastrophe for personal relationships and happiness. I'm not suggesting that you become bland, meaning all things to all people; I'm just suggesting that you think carefully about the things you decide to take a rigid stand on. Just how important are they? Are they really worth jeopardising other relationships? Might it not be that a small compromise now preserves a greater satisfaction later?

Respecting others takes strength

It is a sign not of weakness but of maturity to recognise the merits of others' points of view. This is a concept that gets muddied in the helter-skelter of life and our rush to get what we feel we deserve as soon as possible. In later life you can more easily afford to acknowledge that others deserve a piece of the world too, and that although their ways are not necessarily your ways, they are valid for them. In other words, you can agree to differ, to respect each other's point of view and give each other space. This mature attitude turns potential sources of conflict into things that reinforce rather than threaten relationships. To acknowledge other's viewpoints is not to deny the validity of your viewpoints; I am not telling you to do as others wish, regardless of your own desires. But go that extra step to see if mutually acceptable compromise is possible.

Possible sources of conflict

The following are some reasons why problems might arise at retirement or soon after.

Freedom allows change

In your new status, there is time to reflect on what you are and where you are going. I hope you will do this constructively, and the aim of much of this book has been to help you do it. Your partner may not share your enthusiasm, or they may do exactly the same analysis – and select a direction that takes them away from you. Here is a fundamental truth: change is inevitable, it is likely to be uncomfortable and you must be prepared for this.

You may also not like the implications of changing – perhaps you find that you have less freedom of choice after retirement than you expected, whereas your partner finds that he or she has more freedom. This can be through their personality (they may be more outgoing and adventurous), their health (they may have less arthritis or other debilitating problems) or their opportunities (their previous hobbies, interests and friendships). This mismatch of opportunities could easily lead to deeper resentment. It needs careful handling to ensure that minor resentments do not grow into major objections.

There is more time

While it may not be entirely true that the devil finds work for idle hands, he certainly casts a few loose balls. You have time to reflect on your situation and your options. This is healthy and something you should do, as I have been suggesting. However, being human means that to think is to dream and to dream is to feel dissatisfaction with the status quo. This too is healthy and an impetus to make constructive changes. Clearly it is also a potential source of conflict because dreams do not necessarily coincide – indeed, they are unlikely to do so.

That habit your partner has of leaving the dishes on the table – it was always irritating but, given enough leisure time, it gets to be infuriating. Or the situation where one person is prompt and the other always late; again, what in the past has been no more than a minor irritation can become a major problem.

Does this sound petty? It isn't, for the following reason. Major sources of conflict between you and your partner will probably have led to major rifts already. If some aspects of another's behaviour or lifestyle are completely unacceptable, the chances are you have parted company long ago. So it is precisely the small sources of conflict that are likely to remain and need working on.

How to handle this.

- Be frank about each other's personalities, health and preferences and the difficulties these cause.
- Express any irritations you are feeling, rather than let them smoulder unsaid.
- Look for ways of compromising, for example on outdoor activities and your social life. If you care for each other, a compromise can nearly always be worked out. Only if you value your relationship less than the activities you want to pursue, may there be an unbridgeable rift which threatens your relationship.

Common goals move apart

During your working life your goals are likely to have been broadly shared – the house, money, how to bring up the children. You will probably have had a broad measure of agreement about handling these things, even if part of that agreement was to leave it all to someone else!

All that can change during later life; the framework for this common agreement will inevitably break down. The children leave home, the house is as you like it, money – well, who couldn't do with more? So now what? As you experiment with new freedoms it is more likely that your choices will start to diverge and in this divergence lies possible conflict.

What to do

- Decide on what you both want, on what is essential and what you can compromise about. Remember that you are unlikely to have reached retirement age in a stable partnership without a broad measure of agreement about these quite concrete matters; therefore the chances of significant problems are relatively low. Nor is it likely that you will yearn after new goals which differ greatly from your previous activities – though there are those who sail round the world or want to move to a sunny island, to the consternation of friends and family.

- Take your time. Ironically, what is more likely to cause problems is the realisation that your options are wide open, rather than the options themselves. It could be bewildering to be faced with so much freedom, coupled with the feeling that you have to make a decision quickly. It will take months, even a year or so, to adjust to retirement and it makes sense to defer major decisions until you feel comfortable with your new status. During that time you will find that your goals tend to sort themselves out. The initial rush to do something to prove you are retired will almost certainly give way to a more balanced view about your future actions, so that what might have threatened conflict with your partner may later simply fade away as a source of disagreement.

- Write things down. Keep a list of things that appeal to you, opportunities that seem attractive, things others enjoy, things you read about. Some you may want to experience immediately, others you will forget about unless you keep a note. Even better, start to keep such a list well before retiring. By comparing lists you may see that there is far more overlap in your goals than conflict.

Health issues

Some conflicts you choose, but some fate imposes on you, and health is the major one. As you get older it is unlikely that you will both age at the same biological rate. More likely, one aspect of your health will change faster than others and this can lead to problems, the conflict being between what you want to do and what you are able to do, both individually and together.

Arthritis, heart disease, memory loss, chronic bronchitis – these will impose boundaries on what you can do that will be frustrating for the other, fitter people in your life. This might sound callous, no one ever said that getting older was going to be all easy.

What to do
- Build on love. Humans bond for long periods and history shows that the majority of partners cope with changes in the other, even

where that carries a large emotional or physical cost. It may be more difficult where there is a large age gap, because the older you become, the more stark the physical and mental effects of this become.

- Take time out. If one of you suffers from a disability, look for respite and for any help available. Do everything you can to build protected time into your schedule.
- Sympathise. This sounds obvious, but it can be difficult where someone is suffering from a stroke or Alzheimer's disease, for example, with a major change in personality. It can be easier in the case of something like arthritis or angina, where you can often still maintain a shared lifestyle, though with adjustments.
- Accept anger and resentment. Despite whatever counselling, help and respite you may receive, it would be odd if you didn't still experience frustration from the effects on your own freedom. Hopefully, you will cope with these episodes but some will find the pressure unbearable and leave, although this is remarkably rare.

Children and parents: The filling in the sandwich

You are in the middle of a curiously modern sandwich. Thanks to increasing life expectancy, it is likely that your own parents will be alive during your retirement as well as your own children. This makes for an odd assortment of roles, because you are simultaneously parents to one generation and children to another – at the same time as you are trying to be yourselves and to push your own life forward.

Though these are unavoidable constraints on your freedom, you do have some control on how you deal with them.

As if that was not complicated enough, your relationships will change with time. At the moment you retire, and even for a few years afterwards, your children may still be dependent on you financially and emotionally. Hopefully your own parents will still be independent at this stage, though as time passes they are likely to call on you more. In this curious set-up, both you and your children will be looking at your parents as a kind of role model of how later life may develop. Meanwhile you and your parents will be looking back a generation, trying to make sense of how life has gone up to now and what arrangements are needed to keep things as good as possible for as long as possible.

There will be subtleties about this view. I hope it will include pride and a sense of achievement in whatever careers people have made or are entering into; shared satisfactions and disappointments; some major regrets, for reasons that one generation may not yet be ready to share with another generation; wisdom that older generations may want to share with younger ones; and dreams that each generation wants to share with the other but feels too inhibited to do so.

So what might seem an unhealthy and incompatible mix of generations can and should be seen as an amazing conglomeration of experience and wisdom that should be shared positively.

What prevents this? The old problems of past habits of behaviour and of relationships which have become fixed in their style over many years. Really it is a question of how to escape from the roles you have all held over the years – if you want to. For example, your own parents may greatly resent being called by their Christian names even while you are encouraging your own children to address you in this more informal way. And it is an illusion to imagine that you can cast aside the relationships within a family, or even that it is necessary to do so.

In an ideal world each generation would enjoy its own particular freedoms without interfering with those of any other generation. In the real world this is unlikely to happen all of the time, though there is no reason why it shouldn't happen for much of the time, if you ensure that your freedom is respected as much you respect the demands others make on you.

What to do

- Try to relate to both your parents and your children as adults. Rather than talking about family and upbringing, ask them about their working lives, their hobbies and their world-view. Offer to share your own experiences, making it clear that you are not trying to impose your views on them.
- Offer advice carefully. Your experiences are important but derive from a world that is unavoidably different from that experienced

by either your parents or your children.
- Focus on what has gone right, not wrong. It is important not to dwell on the past, where nothing can be done or where all possible lessons have been learnt. Rather than contribute to continuing resentments, focus on good memories – of holidays, gatherings and celebrations.

Separation, divorce, losing touch

Despite your best efforts, even very long-standing relationships can still fall apart. Within the family, complete breakdown is unlikely because of the array of ties that bind – financial and emotional. However, though the relationship may not break, it can be very uncomfortable and brittle. This is such a widespread phenomenon that it is almost accepted as the norm that there will be problems within families as everyone gets older. Indeed, without them there would not be much fiction or film.

Your relationship with ageing parents is likely to be the most uncomfortable, if you resent them as they become increasingly dependent, memories fail and personalities change. In time their welfare may pose important restraints on your own freedom of action, as you sort out their housing and their care.

Love, hate, duty

These are the three styles in which these tasks can be done. They are not mutually exclusive – we are talking here about real people and not saints. So actions that start off in love may go through periods of hate before settling as duty. Vice versa too: actions that you start with deep resentment may grow into grudging acceptance and eventually into love for the individual.

If possible, you should start from the position of love or, failing that, duty. Whatever your feelings about the important others in your life – lovers, children, spouses, parents – you owe them for many years of satisfaction and it is, I believe, wrong to ignore that hinterland. This is a concept of duty that does not rest easily in the attitudes of the late twentieth and early twenty-first centuries, but I believe it is the healthy attitude.

Why? To put it at its most selfish, because one day you will be relying on someone else's care and attention and the best way of ensuring that that care is delivered willingly is to have striven to deliver your care with fondness and duty. At its most altruistic, we take it as self-evident that parents are owed a duty of care by their children, almost regardless of whatever the previous relationship may have been.

This is so self-evident that there is a danger of introducing a sense of religious commitment. That is not my intention, but it is surely better to build and maintain relationships through love or, at worst, through duty rather than in a spirit of resentment or hate.

When relationships break down

What can be done in these circumstances? Are you faced with divorce, separation and estrangement? If so, what needs to be done?

- First, have all issues been considered objectively. Have you honestly explored what has led to the breakdown in the relationship, acknowledging that you may bear as much responsibility as others?
- Can you be sure that the other side knows your honest point of view?
- Can the reasons for the breakdown be fixed? Can you fix it yourself with effort and honesty? Can you accept that it may be fixable by an outsider if not by yourself?
- Are you certain about the consequences and can you accept them? Do you believe that there will be more to be gained from the breakdown of the relationship than from its continuation?
- Where does your duty lie? In other words is this a relationship that life has saddled you with whatever the cost (family, children)?
- What are you going to do?
- Are there arrangements you should make for the person you are leaving?

In formulating these questions and others, and in order to arrive at a honest answer, you will probably need outside help – after all, if it was going to be easy to break the relationship you would not be reading this, you would have done it already. That outside help may be a friend or member of the family, a religious adviser or doctor. It may be a professional counsellor, trained to help you see the whole problem and all the options for a solution.

Case study

Barbara and Henry had appeared to be an ideal couple: supportive, sociable, reliable. Outsiders had never been aware of the difficulties within their relationship, based on a gradually declining mutual affection that had been replaced by companionship only. Comfortable as that was, it was hardly an appealing prospect for the rest of their lives. As they approached retirement they both realised that they would be faced with a choice: to continue in a façade of a marriage or to go their separate ways.

The problem was that they had many things in common and held in common affection – children, grandchildren, friends. It worried them greatly that, in separating, one or other of them might lose touch with these people in their lives.

They found it impossible to discuss these matters with any of their friends or family; they felt that one crack in the façade would lead to total collapse. So they decided to go to a counsellor for an objective outside opinion. The counsellor was non-judgemental, almost to the point of frustration. Nevertheless they realised that they were being led to form their own conclusions, as they would have to live with them. They had to consider who were the most important people in each other's lives and they had to accept that inevitably they would lose some friends and relations. They concentrated on the relationships they valued most highly and thought through how to give these the news of their separation. Thus for close family they decided it was best to give the information in a meeting, with both of them putting their reasons. With certain other relations and friends they decided it would be best to have a private conversation, one to one.

Their hope was to keep things as civilised as possible; this worked with most people but some took great offence and others sided with either Barbara or Henry, refusing to see the other's point of view. They found it worked best to put the reasons in terms of their personal needs rather than dwell on any mutual difficulties.

Their separation was a bruising affair, despite their best plans. While there was much sympathy from friends, close family found themselves siding with one parent or the other. There was a period of estrangement with one of their children who refused to have anything to do with either of them.

It took two years for the dust to settle, by which time both had found other relationships and were formalising a divorce. Barbara and Henry remained on good terms, though both admitted to doubts about whether they had done the right thing. They could just have turned a blind eye to each other's lives; this way was, they felt, fundamentally more honest despite the storms it had caused.

7

How Ageing Affects
Body and Mind

Though much is taken, much abides.

Tennyson, 'Ulysses'

What is ageing?

This is a surprisingly difficult question to answer. Ageing is not an obvious feature of most other life forms, in the sense that there are few species that achieve anything like their potential life-span. Most species die prematurely through disease, predators and accidents. Even for human beings it is only relatively recently that social and medical advances have allowed more than a small minority to live into advanced years, let alone into old age. However, once people achieve a certain age, it seems that they can look forward to a good life expectancy. It may come as a surprise to learn that the life expectancy of someone in their mid-60s (about 20 years) has only increased by two years since the middle of the nineteenth century.

The real gains in life expectancy are not through improved care of illnesses affecting the over-65s. The real gain is from improved treatment of illnesses well before that age, illnesses that previously prevented people from achieving old age. These treatments include improved child healthcare and better treatment of infectious illness in childhood and early adult life.

The cells which make up the body are continuously reproducing, even in old age; the rate of reproduction is greatest in the cells of the blood, skin and the lining of the intestinal system. Relatively non-changing cells include those of the kidney, brain, heart, muscle and lens of the eye. This fact explains some of the more common problems of old age, such as brain failure and kidney failure.

So what other mechanisms can account for ageing? There are several theories, none of which give the whole answer, which will no doubt prove to be some combination of all of them.

Heredity

Genetic factors are significant but relatively modest in their importance and interact with lifestyle and environment. However, several strands of evidence suggest that genes do play a role. Studies of twins have shown a genetic influence on age-associated diseases such as cancers and atherosclerosis, and people with the genetic disorder Down's syndrome show features of early ageing. A few genes, such as those associated with Alzheimer's disease and osteoporosis, are of particular interest. Certain rare genetic disorders, such as progeria, cause premature ageing but it is uncertain how this relates to normal ageing. And of course different species have different life-spans.

Gender

The differences between the life expectancy of men and women are closing; women used to outnumber men significantly in later life. Though this is still broadly the case, the gap is narrowing. Why should this be? Figures in the twentieth century might be skewed by the premature deaths of men in wars and industrial and road accidents. These factors coincided with the spectacular fall in the deaths of women in childbirth and pregnancy, and so a gender gap emerged. As the importance of those factors fades, so the gap decreases.

Changes in the molecules of the body

This theory suggests that over time the vital molecule DNA – which is the blueprint for making all the other proteins in the body – gradually becomes damaged, causing higher numbers of chromosome abnormalities in older cells. The accumulation of damage is from failure to repair damage to the DNA from heat, cold, chemicals and the effects of natural radiation (cosmic rays and background radio-activity). Each time cells divide, errors could creep into the structure of DNA.

There is great interest at present in what are called free radicals. These are oxygen and other atoms in a particular form which is highly reactive and may damage vital proteins. In particular, free radicals could interfere with the working of the mitochondria – the minute objects within each cell which provide the power to keep the cell running. The body has several biochemical mechanisms to counteract these free radicals, leading to speculation that it is the decreased efficiency of these systems that allows increasing damage. This is why there is so much current focus on eating foods that contain natural anti-oxidants which may counteract the free radicals. Such foods include citrus fruit, for vitamins E and C, and selenium from nuts.

Another process suspected to cause ageing is called glycation; over time molecules of sugar gradually attach themselves to various vital proteins, reducing their efficiency. This theory is based on the observation that diabetics show several features of early ageing of their blood vessels.

A biological clock

This theory holds that cells are naturally preset to last only a certain length of time, perhaps by putting a limit on the number of divisions a cell can make. Or it may be via some other restriction on how long cells can live through their ability to produce energy and deal with damage or disease. This theory created excitement by suggesting the existence of one gene responsible for setting these limits. Once found, perhaps this 'ageing gene' could be switched off. Unfortunately (or perhaps fortunately) the situation has proved far more complex; there is no current evidence for a single gene.

How the body ages

Whatever the underlying causes, the consequences of ageing are all too clear. We can look at this system by system.

Connective tissue

This is a network of cells, mainly within the skin, that supports other structures such as nerves and blood vessels. Connective tissue (much, though not all, of which is called collagen) gives skin its elasticity and form. Over time collagen loses its elasticity and this contributes to thin, delicate skin, wrinkling and similar age-related skin changes. Though this is important, most skin changes are from ultraviolet light – see the section below on skin.

Muscle and stamina

By stamina we understand the ability to keep going; generally this is a physical rather than a mental ability, though there is overlap. Stamina is influenced by muscle power, output from the heart and the ability of tendons and ligaments to withstand prolonged use. After the age of 40 it is estimated that the output of the heart (how much blood it can pump per minute) falls by about 1 per cent a year and the lungs become less elastic and therefore less efficient at responding to oxygen demands

Muscle power tends to peak in early adult life. With training it can stay at that level to the age of 40 to 45 but thereafter starts to decrease quite fast; for example, by the age of 65 someone could have lost 10 per cent of the bulk of muscle they had as a young adult and that will cause loss of stamina. By middle age even trained athletes cannot compete with people 15 to 20 years younger; for example 'veteran' in tennis has come to mean 40 for women and 45 for men.

Regular exercise slows the loss of muscle and bone but does not prevent it. By the age of 80, most people have lost half of their peak muscle mass and replaced it with fat. Metabolism declines, so food intake needs to be reduced from middle age, especially of fats, carbohydrates and alcohol.

Vision

By middle age, colour vision and night adaptation have deteriorated noticeably; this, coupled with changes in focusing and possibly cataracts, makes for less efficiency in sight. This is why as you get older you need better illumination, colours may seem less vivid and you are less aware of your environment. Other conditions that especially affect ageing eyes are cataracts, macular degeneration (deterioration of the light-sensitive retina), glaucoma and dry eyes. The eyes gradually look sunken because of loss of the surrounding fat within the orbits of the skull.

Over time the lens of the eye becomes more fibrous and less flexible; its ability to focus on close objects deteriorates till you have to hold objects further away to read them comfortably. If you were short-sighted in your youth you become long-sighted as you get older, hence the need for so many older people to wear glasses. Poorer vision is one reason why older people are more at risk of falling.

Hearing

It is so common to lose hearing efficiency as you get older that it is virtually normal. The usual type of hearing loss is called presbyacusis, where what is lost is the ability to hear higher-pitched sounds. Since these are the sounds involved in speech, the outcome is difficulty in following conversations, hearing on the phone and hearing in other social settings.

There is a genetic element in this, and it is made worse by noise damage. However, the bulk of the deterioration is from gradual loss of efficiency in all the various intricate components involved in hearing, from stiffening of the bony connections and poorer blood flow within the inner organs to an increased tendency to build up hard wax.

The result of all this is more than simple difficulty in hearing; the mechanisms of the ear are also vital to localizing sound (where is that coming from?) and balance. So disorders of balance, with giddy spells and dizziness, are extremely common, together with deterioration of localization of direction. Another common effect is tinnitus, a constant ringing in the ears, the cause of which is not entirely understood.

Though loss of vision is serious, in some ways loss of hearing is worse because it can lead to isolation and loss of social experience and so to depression. Fortunately, most people with hearing problems can be helped.

Heart and circulation

The heart actually remains remarkably efficient at pumping blood throughout most of life. Where it gets let down is by its own blood supply and by loss of elasticity in the arteries into which it outputs blood. Coronary artery disease is an epidemic in the Western world, the cause of much disability, loss of function, disease and death. It arises through the clogging of the arteries by greasy deposits of fats (atheroma), which makes the walls more liable to rupture and blood clots more likely to form within the heart.

The heart does become less able to respond to exercise and stress, leaving you feeling breathless or tiring more easily. High blood pressure is extremely common, increasing the risks of a stroke, heart failure and kidney damage. Surprisingly, low blood pressure is extremely common too, caused by loss of elasticity in the walls of arteries, which allows blood pressure to drop greatly between heartbeats. The effect is called postural hypotension and is a frequent reason for dizziness and light-headedness among the elderly, especially when first getting up from a chair or from bed.

Importantly, the ageing heart is subject to disturbances of rhythm through disease of the electrical pathways that make the heart beat. A common form is atrial fibrillation, where the heart beats in a fast, irregular, and therefore inefficient, pattern. Another common condition is heart block; here the electric signal to beat fails to transmit to all the heart muscle, which therefore beats at its own slow and inefficient in-built rate. These and many other abnormal rhythms are treatable with medication and pacemakers.

Lungs

Over time the lungs lose their elasticity so that maximum breathing capacity decreases. The lungs have a natural protective system of cells with hairs which sweep impurities out. With age this mechanism gets less efficient, making the older lung more prone to infection and less efficient at its basic job of getting oxygen into the bloodstream and carbon dioxide out. All these unavoidable changes are made much worse by the avoidable factors of cigarettes and pollution. In addition the ability to breathe deeply declines as the ribs become stiffer and as the chest shrinks through the effects of osteoporosis on the spine.

The overall effect is that older lungs have less reserve capacity to cope with extra demands of exertion and exercise. In short, you get out of breath more easily. Again this can be combated; exercise allows possible improvement in lung function probably right into advanced old age. The lungs do become much more liable to infection, which explains why chest infections are so much more common in the elderly and can be so much more serious than in a younger person with better defences and reserves of lung capacity.

Kidneys

The kidneys are unsung heroes of the body, quietly and efficiently filtering impurities from the blood, with urine as their most obvious product. They have other important roles in regulating blood pressure, controlling the amount of fluid in the body, dealing with calcium balance (and therefore bone formation) and conserving the minerals vital to metabolism such as sodium and potassium.

The kidneys comprise millions of units called nephrons, each of which is a tiny biological filtration device. The kidneys have tremendous over-capacity; this is why a kidney donor can survive perfectly well with their sole remaining kidney. However, by somewhere between 60 and 80 years of age kidney function declines by about half. This is normally still enough to cope with the body's requirements, but it leads to some inevitable effects as you get older. One is an increased risk of fluid loss and fluid overload, for example in heat or through not drinking enough. Another is loss of potassium in the urine, which can lead to a generalised weakness of muscles.

Poorer kidney function is another reason why the elderly are more liable to giddiness and low blood pressure on standing, because their kidneys are not able to react to changes in posture as efficiently as when younger. Furthermore, many medications can affect the kidneys, and doctors have to take this into account when selecting or adjusting medication. Common drugs that affect the kidneys are diuretics (water tablets) and ACE inhibitors given for blood pressure or heart failure, and anti-inflammatory drugs to control the pain of arthritis. Kidney failure as such is a relatively uncommon problem in the elderly, unless it is precipitated by other serious illness such as a stroke, heart disease or after serious accidents and major operations.

Diabetes

This is an extremely common disease in later life affecting at least 5 per cent of the over-60s, rising to 10 per cent or more in certain populations. So-called mature onset diabetes is a less dramatic event than in younger age groups and is suspected on the basis of increased thirst, increased passage of urine, possibly weight loss and a general sense of lack of wellbeing. Many cases are discovered by pure chance through testing of urine for sugar or investigation of other illnesses. The importance of diabetes is that it affects so many organs of the body – the heart, blood vessels, kidneys, eyes and skin. Careful control of blood sugar reduces the risks of damage to these organs and this can be achieved by diet, tablets and (less commonly in the elderly) injections of insulin. The chances of developing diabetes are increased by being overweight; we return to the theme of obesity and overeating on page 123.

Autonomic nervous system failure

Here is another relatively unsung system whose deterioration with age causes several common problems. The autonomic nervous system works at an unconscious level outside normal voluntary control. This is unlike the more familiar voluntary nervous system through which we can control the movement of muscles in our limbs, face and, to some extent, our bowels and bladder. The autonomic systems function automatically, responding to stimuli we are rarely aware of such as temperature (opening pores, sweating, raising hair), digestion (switching the glands responsible for digesting food on and off) and energy control. Much of this is in conjunction with the endocrine system of hormones. Other functions are on the fringes of consciousness such as increasing heart rate and heart power in response to stress or exercise, co-ordinating swallowing and digestion and controlling bladder and bowel actions at a level before they reach our conscious attention.

The most important effects of an ageing autonomic system are on control of blood pressure, temperature and bowel and bladder function.

Blood pressure control

Getting up and lying down are major challenges to overall blood pressure; when you stand, nearly two pints of blood literally pools in your legs. The autonomic system normally adjusts rapidly and effortlessly to make the necessary changes to blood vessels and heart rate in order to keep a steady blood pressure at these times. With age the control gets less efficient, leading to dizziness and light-headedness on standing. This is not helped by other factors such as weaker, stiffer muscles and joints, less efficient organs of balance within the ear and loss of elasticity in arterial walls. Also many drugs for the control of high blood pressure, depression or other conditions can increase the drop in blood pressure on standing. This is why poor balance is so widespread in the older population.

Temperature

Each winter brings tragic stories of elderly people who become hypothermic and are found unconscious or even dead due to the effects of cold. Autonomic failure is one important reason: the body loses the ability to compensate for a fall in temperature by mobilising more energy, closing down skin blood vessels through which heat is lost and other strategies. Shivering becomes less efficient and there is a generally lower rate of metabolism. To this can be added self-neglect, poor food intake, loss of the mobility needed to get food or reach warmth and possibly less sensitivity to a warning fall in the outside temperature.

Hyperthermia is the opposite of hypothermia; here people get too hot because their sweating mechanism is inefficient, as well as through the effect of the other mobility factors mentioned above. Significant numbers of the elderly risk hyperthermia during heat-waves, leading to collapse, dehydration, low blood pressure, chemical imbalance and kidney problems. Death can occur (though usually only in very hot countries), mainly from heart attacks or strokes.

Bladder and bowel function

Though disease can, of course, affect these functions, the changes are often due to failure in the autonomic nervous system leading to incontinence and/or difficulty in bowel and bladder control. Incontinence especially of urine, affects very large numbers of the elderly – surveys suggest some 12 per cent of women and 6 per cent of men over 65 years of age. Often relatively simple treatment is available via medication or, failing that, there is a large range of unobtrusive incontinence pads, sheaths and in-dwelling catheters.

Incontinence of the bowels is much less common and even more embarrassing and socially isolating than urinary incontinence. It is far more often associated with brain disorders, strokes and dementia (assuming that bowel disorders such as bowel cancer have been excluded). Most causes are in fact the result of constipation blocking normal bowel action so that faeces leak past the constipated bowel – so-called overflow incontinence. So, paradoxically, the treatment is often regular laxatives and bowel enemas.

Skin

Think of aged skin and you think of thin, wrinkled skin with discoloured patches, perhaps easy bruising and minor injuries taking much longer to heal, with a high risk of turning into chronically inflamed ulcers. This is only partly due to ageing; we have already mentioned loss of connective tissue in the skin making the under-surface thinner and more wrinkled. In fact, most of the more obvious skin changes are due to the years of exposure to sun, wind and ultraviolet light. These are not strictly speaking caused by ageing, but are akin to the weathering of an old house. True age-related changes are less moisture in the skin and less of the natural lubricants produced by the sweat glands. It is all these factors taken together which account for the dry, wrinkled, lax skin of the elderly.

Old skin is liable to cancerous changes, again not through ageing alone but through years of exposure to radiation. This is why the risks of skin cancer (and prematurely aged skin) are much higher in fair-skinned people living in high sunshine areas such as Australia and the southern United States of America.

The same environmental effects account for prominent blood vessels on the cheeks. Bruising probably occurs because blood vessels are more fragile and less supported by surrounding connective tissues and so tear easily.

Apart from the cosmetic effects and the possibility of skin cancers, the main problem with older skin is its dryness. This causes itching, which can be helped by moisturizing creams.

Bones and joints

Bones are living organisms, highly active organs where the blood is made. All the time bones are being remodelled and reshaped. However, old bones are thin bones and get progressively thinner from the 40s onwards. Many older people will eventually end up with osteoporotic bone, that is to say bones whose central core has become thin and weak, making them more liable to break (see the section on osteoporosis on page 132). This is why a relatively trivial fall in an older person can cause a fracture of the femur (thigh-bone) or the wrists, for example. Sometimes the bones get so thin that they break spontaneously; this commonly happens in the back, with sudden pain, curvature of the back and loss of height.

Meanwhile the strength of muscles and joints similarly declines with age; peak muscle strength is found somewhere between the ages of 20 and 40; thereafter there is a loss of strength and muscle bulk, although this is greatly influenced by regular exercise (see the section on muscle and stamina above). Joints become deformed and stiff with arthritis; this used to be thought of as wear and tear change but is now thought to be a combination of trauma, accidents and genetic influences. Stiff joints mean that you are less able to react to changes in position as you get older, again increasing the risk of unsteadiness and falls and also the chances of spraining a muscle or joint during minor exercise.

The brain

Many people greatly fear how ageing will affect their brain and nervous system. The facts are really quite reassuring. It is true that the brain shrinks as you get older – by your 80s the brain is 7–8 per cent less in volume than in your 20s. But the lifetime loss of the actual neurons (the functional elements of the brain) is only about 3 per cent of the 100,000 million you started with. This does vary greatly in different parts of the brain – the cerebellum (involved in balance and co-ordination of movement) loses neurons at a much faster rate after the late 60s. In addition there is a decrease in concentration of the vital neuro-transmitters; these are the chemical packets that bridge the gap between each neuron. There are also changes in blood flow to the brain (an estimated 20–25 per cent fall at 70 compared to the age of 30). The speed at which the electrical impulse flows along a nerve fibre is 15 per cent slower by 80 than in a 30 year old.

For these reasons the overall speed of reaction time is about 30–40 per cent less in old age, further affected by stiff joints and poorer hearing, vision and balance. On the other hand, reaction time is much better in those taking regular exercise – so deterioration is not inevitable.

People with Alzheimer's disease (senile dementia) show important changes in brain structure, with more tangled cells, loss of branching of other cells and deposits of waste or inflammatory debris between cells. Yet quite how this all links up with the loss of short-term memory in dementia remains unclear. The aged brain is also affected by poor blood-flow, major and minor strokes and (less commonly) brain tumours.

Mental ability

This includes memory, reasoning and personality – aspects of our mental functioning important at all ages, not just as you get older. It is a widespread fear that these will all decline as you get older. It has proved surprisingly difficult to quantify any decline scientifically; this is because simply testing people of different ages becomes confused by their backgrounds, educational opportunities, life experiences, standard of living, access to reading material and so on.

However, there is agreement about a general decline in function once people reach their late 60s. This shows itself in lengthening reaction time to choices, longer time taken to solve problems and shorter attention span (the period of time you can concentrate on a problem). People also feel tired more quickly and find that their attention varies more easily (greater distractibility) and memory worsens.

This might sound depressing; however, the differences between individuals of the same age are much greater than the differences between older and younger people. In other words, there are many people in their 60s and 70s who are more alert and mentally agile than people considerably younger. We shall see in Chapter 9 what can be done to preserve and enhance mental ability.

This situation holds up to about the age of 80. From 80 onwards there is a general decline in function – though again there are still great differences between individuals and we all know of individuals who have preserved an acute mind into their 90s.

Rest and sleep requirements

Sleep problems are to be expected as you get older; for example, it takes longer to get off to sleep (20–25 minutes at 70, against 10 minutes in young adults). Older people find they wake more easily, more abruptly and more frequently and that they stay awake longer. This may be aggravated by other physical problems causing you to wake, such as joint pains, the need to pass urine, a chronic cough or psychological problems such as depression and anxiety. Also if you nap during the day your need for sleep at night is bound to suffer. Even the type of sleep becomes less refreshing with age; there is less time spent in deep Stage 4 sleep (slow wave sleep), when waking is most difficult.

All this means that even the sleep you do get seems less refreshing. Furthermore, older people are less able to 'catch up on sleep' than younger people and therefore feel more severely the effects of losing sleep when travelling, if unwell or if disturbed frequently by some outside problem – neighbours or a grandchild staying with you. Being cold will disturb sleep; so will excess alcohol and caffeine (coffee, tea), snoring and restless legs.

Overall there is a decreased need for sleep as you get older – it is common to sleep for no more than 5–6 hours. You need to preserve what sleep your body asks for, making it as good quality as possible, So get up at a regular hour, rather than dozing in bed, and be active during the day. Ensure a comfortable temperature in the bedroom and exclude noise. Avoid tea or coffee for at least two hours before trying to sleep and try to put worries out of your mind. Remedies are available for restless legs; you should regard sleeping tablets as an absolutely last resort because they do not give a natural sleep and it is easy to become dependent on them.

Psychological health

Older people are less inclined to take risks and tend to a degree of rigidity in their habits and personality. However, older professional people are better at conserving time and energy and distinguishing between critical and less critical tasks. All these contribute to psychological health.

Other factors shown to be important in preserving psychological health include:

• having an adequate standard of living
• financial and emotional security
• good physical health
• regular and frequent social interaction
• the pursuit of personal interests.

Chapters throughout this book deal with these and other factors.

Anxiety, stress and depression

These, common in old age, can become very serious. There is rarely a single identifiable cause for these psychological problems, which may have their roots in a range of issues. These may be loss of partners, friends or children, loss of independence, the effects of chronic illness, the awareness of a decline in your mental and physical abilities, or money and housing problems. On the other hand, older people have often been released from major lifetime stresses such as work, caring for children, adjustment to their own personality and capabilities and socialisation. Increasingly, many of the newly retired find themselves more affluent than at any previous time in their life and with all the freedoms and excitement touched on in other chapters.

Therefore, although these psychological problems are common, they should not be accepted as just an inevitable part of getting older. You will be particularly well placed in having insight into the causes of, say, depression and a more philosophical approach to dealing with it. You can waste less mental energy on asking 'Why me?' and spend more energy on 'What can I do?'

That said, anxiety in particular can sap your mind; common anxieties revolve around such problems as personal safety ('The streets are deadly'), a fear of meeting others, a fear of the new. It has been found that up to 20 per cent of the elderly are suffering from anxiety or depression to some degree.

One difficulty in recognising depression (or admitting it to yourself) is that it can masquerade as an 'understandable reaction' to life events or complaints of pain, tiredness, moodiness, insomnia, even aggression and irritability. It is all too easy to ascribe such feelings to some physical condition and lose sight of the fact that the reaction has become too extreme, too long-lasting, too debilitating. In other words, it has reached a stage where it is a problem in its own right rather than a reasonable consequence of some other, more obvious, condition. This is unnecessary because, as we shall see elsewhere, depression is eminently treatable, as are anxiety and stress.

Use it or lose it

We have seen how there are inevitable declines in ability as you get older. It is important to remember that there are great individual variations in these changes. Even where they are inevitable, you can still influence the rate of change by exercise, exertion and using your mind. So do not despair nor abandon yourself to decay and decrepitude! Use your abilities to the maximum; push yourself to the limits and work on the basis of trying things first, rather than thinking you can't. I go into more detail on this in the following chapter.

113

8

How to Maintain
Your Body and Mind

Dost thou think, because thou art virtuous, there shall be no more cakes and ale?

Shakespeare, *Twelfth Night*

You have reached retirement fit, active, open minded, optimistic. I hope that you can look back on a well-spent working lifetime and happiness from your family, spouse or partner. How can you stay that way for as long as possible?

In even asking this question you are already taking a major psychological step. You are asserting that life after retirement will not necessarily mean decline, decay, shuttered horizons and reduced expectations. It need not be that way at all. It is truly the third age, an age when you can enjoy the material fruits of your labours and the mental fruits of your experiences. The combination is a highly attractive one, where you can determine new horizons, new goals and set yourself new challenges, with the big difference that you are now much more in charge of setting the agenda than at any time for many years. You are the managing director of the rest of your life.

Realistically, there are obstacles to a golden decline which are addressed in many parts of this book. But this is not something that should dominate your thinking; rather, it should be part of the prudent assessment of your situation that I recommend. Even though you may have health problems and relationship difficulties, there are ways of accommodating these in your life rather than being dominated by them.

So where next? You should consider a strategy that will preserve your health for as long as possible. The principles are not difficult, nor are they startling, surprising or even high technology. Hopefully they are already habits that you established when younger and can carry forward with suitable adjustments for getting older. Please note that these are recommendations only. The last thing I want is for you to become obsessional about diet, cholesterol, blood pressure or whatever. Variations from what I recommend should be a source of pleasure and not a reason for anxiety. However, taken as a broad guide to staying healthy, these recommendations will help you maintain yourself at your full potential.

Another point is often overlooked. We live in a psychologically dominated age: an age of endless analysis of motive, mood, emotions and psychological cause and effect. It is of course important to recognise the power of psychological influences – memories of an abused childhood can come back to haunt adults in ways possibly more painful than breaking a leg. But there is a danger of over-psychologising much of what we do, when it is in fact appropriate to say mentally, 'Enough is enough. Now do something, rather than keep thinking things over.'

Healthy eating

It has become a truism that our diet affects our health. Most of us are far more aware about the health implications of what we eat, though still greatly confused about some of the more obscure risks to health such as BSE or genetically modified foods. From all the controversy and confusion, certain healthy principles emerge which are broadly accepted by the authorities. These are:

- a diet low in saturated fats and higher in polyunsaturated fats
- high intake of fibre and fruit
- lowering of salt.

These recommendations are based on studies of international trends in death and illness, covering cancers, heart disease, strokes and overall life expectancy. Typical studies have been how a change of diet in Japan or Hungary over several decades appears to link up with changes in heart disease and cancers.

These studies are very difficult to do and very hard to interpret. For example, along with a Western diet, there will be Western pressures, job insecurity, less exercise, more stress and the breakdown of family support structures. Researchers are aware of these other factors, though their effect defies precise measurement. Still, the surveys do the best they can, which is one reason why medical researchers look with suspicion at health scares which suddenly pronounce on 'the cause of cancer' or heart attacks with a certainty quite unjustified by any research.

Our measures of these influences on health are not very precise; at present there is serum cholesterol (reflecting fat intake) and blood pressure levels (reflecting salt intake and to a lesser extent fat intake). These do not affect health on their own but are influenced by coexisting factors which are thought to amplify the effects of fat and salt. These include smoking, diabetes, personality type, alcohol, obesity and genetic predisposition. To counteract the adverse affects there are polyunsaturated fats, mono-unsaturated fats, avoiding smoking and obesity and anti-oxidants in food. Medical measures, while important, are a 'me-too' measure rather than a be-all and include control of blood pressure and reduction of cholesterol.

Studies have shown just how quickly diet and lifestyle affect cholesterol; for example, the cholesterol levels of Korean recruits to the US army who changed to a Western diet rose to US levels in six months. Conversely, Western recruits to a Zen monastery showed falls in cholesterol in six months to figures similar to those of the indigenous monks. It has not been so easy to show how diet affects blood pressure, because diet varies, but results suggest that changes take a year or more.

So there is little doubt about the importance of diet. But in addition there is little doubt about how quickly dietary changes can make a difference. This means that it is worth moving to a healthier diet even when you are in your 60s or 70s. Beyond that age we just do not know. Current medical opinion sees no proven benefit from reducing cholesterol after the age of 75 – at least not by the use of medication. But dietary change costs little and it would seem only common sense to extend the guidelines for healthy eating into advanced old age.

Nutritional needs

The body's basic requirements are for energy, protein, iron, salts and vitamins, fibre and water.

Energy
This comes from carbohydrates (starch, rice, pasta, bread) and from fat (butter, animal fats, oils). You should aim for a diet low in animal fats, high in polyunsaturated or mono-unsaturated fats such as olive oil and polyunsaturated spreads. Saturated fat should make up no more than about 10 per cent of dietary fat intake.

As you get older you may find you need to eat less energy-giving foods, depending on your level of activity. If you remain active, chances are that your appetite and food intake will alter little as you get older, averaging around 2100–2500 calories a day for men and about 20 per cent less for women. Should you become very sedentary, then your energy requirements will certainly be less and you should adjust your calorie intake to avoid getting overweight.

Protein
This is the building block for muscles and the organs of the body; you still need protein as you get older because there is a continual turnover of the cells in your body. Particularly good sources of protein are cheese, meat, beans, pulses, bread, fish and milk; men need only about 1 gram of protein per kilogram of body weight a day (about 3 oz a day for a 12 stone man), women again 20 per cent less. This is such a modest daily amount that you are unlikely to become protein deficient unless you deliberately follow a very odd diet indeed. In fact most people in the affluent world eat far more protein than the small basic requirement.

Iron
You need iron to make blood cells and to avoid anaemia, but there is no reason to alter your diet as you get older to obtain enough iron. Iron is found naturally in meat and eggs, and is often added to cereals

117

such as cornflakes. As with protein, deficiency is unlikely unless you follow an unbalanced diet. Anaemia, even if iron deficiency appears to be the cause, does worry doctors because of a chance that the anaemia is due to internal blood loss, that is, through bleeding into the stomach from a stomach ulcer or into the bowel from a bowel cancer. Therefore if your doctor finds you are anaemic without some very clear dietary cause, he or she is likely to advise further investigations.

Calcium

There is increasing recognition of the health hazards of osteoporosis and emphasis on its prevention; dietary calcium is important to maintaining strong bones throughout your life. Arguably calcium gets more important the older you are, as the risks from a bone fracture become more serious. Milk and dairy products are good sources of calcium. Aim for 1–1.5g a day.

Vitamin D

This is vital for ensuring healthy bones and it is lack of vitamin D rather than lack of calcium which is more likely to underlie osteoporosis. It may come as a surprise to learn that the body makes most of the vitamin D it needs through the action of sunlight on the skin. Only a relatively small amount of vitamin D comes via the diet and this dietary source only becomes important if you are confined indoors for very long periods of time. Dietary sources of vitamin D are especially milk and dairy products.

Other vitamins and minerals

You will read claims for vitamins C and E, selenium, zinc (required for enzymes and to make cell membranes), potassium, magnesium, manganese, vitamin A, thiamine and iodine, along with a host of others. It is true that lack of these can cause illness and this happens in some parts of the world where diets are extremely restricted. However, in the affluent West deficiency of any of these is unlikely unless you follow an unusually restricted diet. It is enough to ensure you eat fresh fruit and green vegetables daily, remembering that over-cooking vegetables destroys vitamin C and, being soluble, it can get thrown away in water.

That said, it is understandable why many people like to take a vitamin capsule that contains a selection of all the above, feeling that they can then be sure they are getting what they need. Certainly there is no harm in doing this and it may be that some controversial elements are helpful – for example, selenium and vitamins B and E may help prevent heart disease. Read the pack carefully – it should give the recommended daily intake and what the capsules contain. So you can make up your mind about what you need, taking into account your diet and lifestyle; for example, if you are strictly vegetarian, more iron is advisable, and if you stay indoors a lot, more vitamin D and calcium. There is no benefit from taking more than you need – your body will just excrete the excess, benefiting no one but the manufacturer. And it is harmful to take too much of some vitamins and minerals such as vitamin A (leading to liver damage) and calcium (which can cause constipation and abdominal discomfort).

Healthy eating in a nutshell

- Eat fruit, vegetables and starch regularly, five helpings a day, for example, an apple, a banana, a couple of clementines, a few grapes or cherries. A glass of fruit juice counts as one portion, as does a couple of tablespoons of canned fruit, or a helping of any vegetable or salad. Drink low fat milk and yogurts. Increase your intake of soluble fibre such as beans, lentils, pulses, oats, fruit and vegetables. Bread, rice and pasta are particularly good at satisfying appetite whilst providing fibre and carbohydrate. Better to have these and reduce your intake of biscuits and cakes, which are high in sugar and often fat and salt too.
- Use unsaturated fats such as olive oil, low fat spreads, or sunflower oil rather than butter, normal margarine or lard. Even then try to grill or boil food rather than fry it and, of course, choose low fat meat such as chicken.
- Avoid sugar; it's just empty calories that lead to weight gain and tooth decay. Use artificial sweeteners or just readjust your taste, which only takes a few weeks. As it happens a sweet tooth tends to decline anyway as you get older.
- Reduce the amount of salt in the diet. This is especially important if you have high blood pressure; salt is universally used for flavouring but especially in soups, sauces, crisps and biscuits. Try not to

add salt automatically to your food before you even taste it.

Fluid intake

The average adult needs a minimum of 1 litre of water a day, but usually gets much more unnoticed in food – to illustrate this, think of the difference between moist ordinary bread and dry toast. Water really does 'flush the kidneys' because the body dissolves many waste products in water before excreting them. Fluid also helps prevent constipation. Oddly, as you get older you are less likely to feel thirsty, making it more important to drink regularly whether you feel the need or not. In normal circumstances, this is not critical but it is something to bear in mind in hot weather, on holiday in warm climates and after exertion. In this way avoid dehydration with its symptoms of nausea, headache, muscle cramps and more severe symptoms of confusion and collapse.

If you find yourself in these circumstances, take regular drinks whether you feel the need or not. Alcohol does not count – its diuretic effect will push out more fluid than you consume. You need to allow for any medication you are on; certain tablets must be taken with plenty of water, or you may be on diuretic tablets to control heart failure, in which case you should take care not to drink excessively.

Exercise

Exercise is valuable at all ages and there are hardly any circumstances which will prevent you doing some physical exercise. Even if you are immobilised in a chair, or following a stroke, there is nearly always something you can do to tone your muscles and to get your heart racing. But for what? Why do exercise? At a most basic level, humans are made for activity; that's why we have muscles, long limbs, stereoscopic vision and a brain, much of which is devoted to controlling muscular activity, balance and co-ordination. We are made to move and when we do so our muscles maintain their ability, they remain firm rather than flabby. Then there is the heart – that's muscle too and capable of being trained. The trained – exercised – heart has greater reserves of power to cope with unexpected demands –

climbing a hill, a brisk walk, lifting a mattress, carrying heavy shopping.

Exercise uses energy, so it burns up your last meal. Regular exercise is important in weight control: if you eat the same but exercise less you will inevitably start to gain weight – just a few ounces a week maybe, but adding up to serious weight gain over a couple of years. Being overweight carries its own problems and health hazards (see below).

Other advantages of exercise

- Psychological well-being, from a sense of freedom, independence, flexibility of limbs.
- Meeting people – you see your environment, your environment sees you and sees that all is well.
- Cardiovascular toning – regular exercise tones the heart and blood vessels and is proven to reduce the risks of heart disease. Even people with known heart or circulatory problems benefit from exertion, as long as they avoid chest pain or breathlessness.
- Prevention of osteoporosis, by keeping bones strong and by exposure to daylight, so important for the formation of vitamin D.

Convinced? Now, how much?

- Aim to walk for half an hour two or three times a week. That hardly sounds painful. Try to fit a hill or steps into your route, sufficient to raise your pulse rate and make you feel a little out of breath. Even if that is uncomfortable on week one, it will get easier if you keep doing it over just four to eight weeks. If you are new to even such modest exercise, you should build up by walking more slowly for the first five minutes (warming up) and slower again in the last five minutes (warming down). This gives your body the chance to adapt to the changing demands on it. Your goal should be to be able to walk at three to four miles an hour in comfort.
- There will be other routine activities that provide exercise, such as mowing the lawn, gardening and housework. Perhaps you already play sports such as golf, swimming, tennis, or bowls. There

is every reason to continue; naturally you will select with whom you play so that your levels of physical fitness coincide; most sports recognise this and make allowances for veterans. When you go shopping, why not use the stairs rather than the escalator or lift and why not park the car a couple of hundred yards away rather than park right outside the store?

- There are now many exercise classes for older people in halls and swimming pools, or walking groups. These have the advantage of introducing you to exercise in a supervised and graded way, with clear goals for you to achieve. That is over and above the social side and the discipline imposed by knowing that you have a regular date to attend. They may force you to use muscles you never knew you had and would rather not be reminded about and show you what others of your age are capable of achieving. Once you have found your own level, you may wish to go it alone.

- Another advantage of a group is to give you confidence, seeing others with particular illnesses exerting themselves. Such classes are becoming widespread for rehabilitation after heart attacks or heart surgery, proving to individuals that activity, even strenuous activity, is entirely possible after such serious illness.

What to avoid

- Do not take up strenuous sports without building up to them carefully. Maybe you did play tennis once, 25 years ago. By all means start playing again, but be very cautious about running, sudden bursts of exertion, twisting your joints and falls. Bear in mind the value of warming up and warming down. Jogging, running and cycling are not a good idea, because of the strain it puts on your joints through the impacts. Unless you have done them for a long time, you should not mark your retirement by purchasing jogging gear or a mountain bike; build up to these levels of activity carefully.

- When you do take up exercise after a long break, be alert to certain symptoms. These include unusual breathlessness, chest discomfort, pains in the leg muscles, or dizziness. Stop if you get these symptoms and seek medical advice, as they may be symptoms of heart and circulatory disease.

- Take extra care in cold weather, which puts extra demands anyway on your heart and lungs. It may seem a good idea to shovel away snow from a drive but take it easily and rest frequently. Be careful of walking during frosty weather and ensure that you have non-slip footwear with a good grip and dress appropriately.

And finally...
• Don't stop. Keep mobile and exercising for as long as you can, because if you do stop you will go out of condition quickly and find it harder to re-establish your previous level of fitness.

How to control your weight

Food is, or should be, a pleasure whatever your age; maybe even more pleasurable as you get older with the increased opportunity to linger over meals, savour food and make eating more of a social occasion than it was previously. Herein lies a problem, because we humans seem unable to stop when we have had enough. Perhaps because eating fulfils several functions, we carry on eating way beyond the point of meeting any conceivable bodily need. Couple this with a reduction in mobility and exercise, and there is the almost certainty of weight gain.

Middle-aged spread is common but it need not be inevitable as long as you keep a prudent eye on your diet. And this is important not just for the aesthetics of how you look but because of various health and personal consequences. These include an increased risk of diabetes, heart disease and osteo-arthritis and all the consequences flowing from them. Then again there is the poor self-image if you let yourself run to fat, the discomfort in summer from sweating and the increased tendency to skin rashes and leg ulcers. A gloomy prospect, but it need not be that way; you owe it to yourself to keep an eye on your weight for your future well-being.

Telling whether you are overweight

The simplest signs are the best – the skirt that has 'shrunk', the shirt that was once loose but which now wraps itself around a straining body like a second skin. Make a note of your weight when your clothes feel comfortable and when they start to feel strained; the difference may be just a few pounds.

A more scientific method is to calculate your body mass index, because this makes allowance for body build. Measure your height in metres and your weight in kilograms. The Body Mass Index (BMI) is weight divided by the square of height. For example, take a woman weighing 70 kg (11 stone) and 1.63m (5 foot 4 inches) tall. Her BMI is $70 \div (1.63 \times 1.63) = 26.3$. This is mildly overweight. Desirable BMIs for women are in the range 19–24, for men 20–25; this does rise with age, for example above the age of 65 an acceptable BMI would be 24–29, which does give comfortable leeway. A BMI a little above those figures signals definite overweight, though not a major health hazard.

BMIs much above 30 signal important obesity about which you should do something to avoid the health risks of heart disease, diabetes and stroke, as these risks are quite significantly raised if you are more than 20 per cent over ideal weight. There is also evidence of an increased risk of certain cancers (prostate and bowel in men, breast, ovary and womb in women). The good news is that the converse holds: if you diet back to a desirable weight, your risks of these various illnesses also fall back to the average.

Another method to quick self-assessment is the ratio of waist circumference to hip circumference. Measure your waist and divide that figure by your hip measurement. For women this should be below 0.9, for men below 1.

However you measure it, overweight and obesity are increasingly common; this may obscure the problem because if everyone you know is overweight you may not see your own overweight for what it really is.

Controlling your weight

With so many diet plans available it should be possible to choose one you feel comfortable with. Avoid crash diets that rely on unusual foods and supplements; though these may provide spectacular short-term weight loss, they are not sensible as a long-term routine. You need one that offers a balanced diet and moderate food intake. A balanced diet means one with recommended amounts of carbohydrate, fat, cholesterol, five helpings a day of fruit and vegetables and alcohol in moderation (21–28 units a week for men, 14–21 for women). Avoid excess salt. For most people it is advisable to have breakfast, then mid-morning snack, lunch, mid-afternoon snack, supper and something before going to bed. In retirement it is easy and tempting to snack continuously, often to relieve boredom. This is a certain route to weight gain. If you must snack, do it with healthy fruit and vegetables rather than empty carbohydrates.

In this way you will maintain an ideal weight, something which is easier to do than to diet down from obesity or up from self-neglect. You might have to adjust your diet in the light of significant changes to your exercise ability. If you find you have become less mobile, for example through arthritis, you should reassess what you eat, cutting down on fat and carbohydrate to avoid weight gain.

Some weight control tips

Keep a food diary
Note everything, all drinks, snacks and nibbles; you may be surprised at how much you eat outside regular meal times.

Plan your meals
Do this up to a week ahead; not only does this help in shopping but it allows you to control intake more precisely.

Vary your diet
If you are desperate for a mid-morning snack, make it fruit rather than biscuits; similarly with desserts.

Be aware of your eating habits
Try to concentrate on your food rather than the conversation; don't automatically take second helpings. Use a smaller plate that looks fuller. If you don't feel hungry don't eat, even though it may be lunchtime.

Special diets

The commonest diets are to reduce cholesterol or to control diabetes. Nowadays, these very much overlap; the days of diabetic diets that excluded normal food and sugar are long gone. Your doctor or dietician can supply appropriate guidelines and monitor your response. Otherwise the likeliest reason to have to diet is if you are overweight but need an operation, typically gall bladder removal or hip replacement. Here again you should be supplied with a target weight and diet guideline. It is hard to imagine circumstances where you might have to go on a crash diet, as people do when younger.

Whatever the reason for dieting, life would be dull indeed if not marked by the occasional binge. There is absolutely no need to feel guilty for letting yourself go at times, as long as you realise what you are doing and accept that some measurements may worsen for a few days afterwards, for example blood sugars if you are diabetic.

Rapid weight changes

Be alert to weight changes without any obvious cause, as both rapid weight loss and weight gain may be pointers to illness. See also 'When to seek help – a summary of warning symptoms and signs' on page 142.

How to keep your emotions healthy

Entering into retirement and beyond takes you into novel areas of emotional expression. Freed from the constraints of a working hierarchy or a traditional nuclear family, you can find yourself able to express emotions more freely than you may have done since adolescence. A great feeling, a healthy outlook, but with this freedom you should be sensitive to the reactions of others. Major emotions you may need to handle are:

- Love
- Dislike
- Fear
- Apprehension
- Irritability
- Frustration
- Envy
- Pride.

Of course none of these is unique to retirement; it is the freedom of expression that is unusual. To a large degree you will already express these emotions in the consistent and predictable way which goes towards what is recognised as your personality – that sum of your emotional tone, interests, intelligence, beliefs and experience which is unique to yourself. However, freed from restraint, any aspect of your personality can get out of check. Here are some examples.

- You feel you do not see enough of your children or grandchildren
- You find your partner starts to irritate you despite your basic affection for him or her
- You start to brood about the success of others
- You become more spontaneous and get irritable because others cannot share your spur of the moment plans.

Now be reassured: so far, so normal. Test out your freedoms; seek the emotional comforts you desire. Yet do not lose sight of the fact that for many of your social circle, life has to follow the demanding routine to which you yourself were tied not so long ago. While you have the freedom, they still have restrictions and their own agendas and demands to follow. And after the first flush of excitement at retiring, there is bound to be a point when excitement goes off the boil, or is taken off the boil by outside influences – money, health, relationships, or change in society.

Warning signs that your emotions are getting out of hand are:

- Brooding over things you cannot change
- Losing interest in people and activities
- Sleep disturbed by worry
- Apprehension about going out
- An exaggerated fear of crime or personal safety
- Increasing preoccupation with your state of health
- Loss of libido (sexual interest)
- Increasing irritability.

These are features of depression and anxiety, extremely common at all ages but especially common in retirement. The chances are that outsiders will bring this to your attention before you admit it to yourself.

What should you do?

- Initially talk about how you feel to those who are important in your life. It is surprising what simple misapprehensions can underlie a mood, through failure to see another's viewpoint or fears simply spiralling out of control. This is not illness; this is human complexity.
- Write down what makes you feel stressed, anxious or unhappy – the situations, the people, the responsibilities. Perhaps it will prove to be one or two things that you should concentrate on dealing with, or even avoiding.
- Give yourself space: call it time out, protected time, quality time, but make it time for yourself. It can be as simple as taking a walk every day, or arranging a regular day out with friends.
- Know what relaxes you and do it. This may be reading a book, taking some exercise, having a bath, having a glass of wine. Know what works for you and use it in a planned, regular way.
- Physical exertion can help by diverting your mind and giving a sense of well-being; even simple stretching and deep breathing exercises a few times a day will do this.
- If things fail to respond to these techniques, thought and discussion, consider consulting a counsellor or your doctor; you may be slipping into a depressive illness. Or there may be aspects of your life coming back to goad your emotional stability now that the rest of the mayhem of life is diminished.

Check-ups, their advisability and value

Is it a good idea to see a doctor on a regular basis, even though you are well? What is the value in this, if any? What is the doctor's reaction likely to be? Should you go to well man or well woman clinics?

The worried well

Doctors recognise a group of people who keep worrying about their health despite having no obvious health problems. This is based on the observation that those who present to doctors for check-ups are often those who do not need them, because they are already health conscious and therefore follow an active life with a good diet and avoid excesses of alcohol and cigarettes. Such individuals may require constant reassurance about each new symptom; generally doctors are happy to do this, but it is reasonable to expect people to be selective about the symptoms they take to their doctor.

There is another group who see themselves as entitled to medical advice regardless. These do irritate doctors, at least within the NHS framework where resources are so limited. Impervious to reassurance and sceptical of advice, such individuals can cause friction as they use up resources on pointless investigations and second opinions. If you feel you are falling into the second category, you might want to consider how reasonable your demands actually are; you may be told that the NHS can take your enquiries only so far, and then you will have to seek further opinions privately.

Unmet need

This is a quite different category; these are people whose lifestyle is medically unsafe, who drink to excess and smoke, fail to take adequate exercise and ignore health advice. On the whole doctors are sympathetic to such individuals and will continue to offer lifestyle advice; ultimately, however, your health rests in your own hands.

Some worthwhile checks

Retirement does mark a watershed and it is a reasonable point at which to have a basic check-up. This will normally include the following.

Blood pressure check

Everyone has blood pressure; it is just the pressure within the arterial system that propels blood around the body, just like a water pump forces water round a central heating system. Blood pressure tends to rise with age because the walls of the arteries become more rigid and the nervous control of blood vessels becomes less efficient.

High blood pressure predisposes to heart disease, strokes and kidney trouble. Treatment is worthwhile whatever your age; some evidence suggests that blood pressure control is more important the older you are, in terms of preventing strokes. You cannot tell whether your blood pressure is raised unless you have it measured. It is a myth that high blood pressure causes headaches or tiredness; this only holds for exceptionally raised pressures, which do require urgent treatment.

A finding of high blood pressure does not imply immediate treatment; you will need to have it rechecked over a few weeks before the doctor decides whether treatment is necessary. During this time your doctor will probably arrange tests to see how your blood pressure is affecting your body. These include an ECG (electrical recording of your heart) to see if there is evidence of strain on your heart; blood tests of kidney function and cholesterol; and a urine test for sugar and protein (a sign of kidney damage). The results of these tests will help to decide whether to treat blood pressure, what medication might be suitable and how vigorously to treat it.

How is blood pressure treated? A first step is to reduce excessive salt intake and to get to an ideal weight – your doctor will advise what to aim at. This can reduce slightly raised blood pressure to a normal reading. Then there is medication, with a vast array of possible drugs and combinations of drugs. About 60 per cent of people can have their blood pressure controlled by one drug; the commonly used ones are bendrofluazide, a beta blocker or a calcium antagonist. About 40 per cent need a combination of two or even three drugs to get good control. This may call for less widely used drugs such as ace inhibitors, alpha blockers, etc. The exact choice is rather complex and takes into account other medical problems and the results of blood tests; for example, an ace inhibitor might be a first choice treatment if you are diabetic or have evidence of heart strain.

Often it takes many months to find a treatment that is effective without causing unacceptable side effects. Once found, you will need a review every few months and occasional blood tests.

Tests for diabetes

Diabetes is an inefficiency in how the body handles sugar, the fuel from which the body makes most of its energy. Much of the food you eat either already contains glucose or else is digested by the body into glucose, which is then stored as a reserve of energy. Glucose circulates in the bloodstream but can only get inside cells if allowed to do so by the hormone insulin. As you get older that system becomes less efficient, either through lack of production of insulin or inefficient release of insulin. The result is a high level of circulating sugar which damages the walls of blood vessels. Diabetes therefore has effects throughout the body: it brings risks of heart disease, kidney disease, poor vision and skin infections as well as causing general tiredness and a sense of being under par. It is extremely common after the age of 60, affecting 2–5 per cent of that age group, many of whom would not know they had diabetes without a test.

The simplest test is on a sample of urine using a chemically impregnated testing strip that detects sugar. It takes under a minute to do the test. A more sensitive test is on blood, but that is not usually needed at a check-up unless the doctor suspects diabetes already or you have other important health problems such as heart disease or high blood pressure.

The treatment of diabetes is not difficult in principle – just a good diet with control over weight, how much sugar and carbo-hydrate you eat and blood tests to check control. A minority of people need medication to control blood sugar and an even smaller minority have to go on to insulin.

There is no such thing as mild diabetes; if detected you should take control seriously because it is a major risk for future problems.

Glaucoma

This is another quite common condition that will generally be missed without a test. It results from increased pressure of the fluids in the eye and affects 0.5–1 per cent of this age group. There is a family tendency: if a close relative has glaucoma you should have regular checks from the age of 40. Otherwise let your optician check the pressure of your eyes every three years – it simply involves a puff of air on each eye, from which the internal pressure can be calculated. The symptoms of glaucoma include poor night vision, haloes around lights at night and a restriction of your field of vision, as if you were looking through a tube (so-called 'tunnel vision'). Unfortunately, by the time you get such symptoms the condition is already far advanced and damage may have been done, hence the sense of regular screening.

Cholesterol

Cholesterol is a much-hyped measurement, easy to get obsessional about. However, it is at present the best marker we have for the risk of heart disease, so it is worth having a blood test at some time well before the age of 60. If your cholesterol is raised, the first step is to attempt to control it by diet – essentially by reducing butter, dairy products and fatty meats and a generally healthy diet. Medication is available to further reduce cholesterol but the need for this requires careful evaluation by your doctor, taking into account your blood pressure, blood sugar, family history of heart disease and, crucially, whether you smoke or not. People on medication need regular tests. Otherwise it is worth having your cholesterol rechecked every three to five years. It is not yet known how worthwhile it is to treat raised cholesterol beyond the age of 75 – discuss the latest findings with your doctor.

Osteoporosis

There is no simple test for osteoporosis and a simple physical check-up will not detect it. For that you need X-rays (with a radiation risk) or a bone scan (expensive and not widely available on the NHS). It is a fact of life that everyone over the age of 60 is at risk of osteoporosis, women more so than men. Rather than having expensive tests, it makes more sense to follow a lifestyle that will maintain bone density, reserving tests for those who are at particular risk or who already have symptoms suggestive of osteoporosis. These include early osteoporosis in parents and siblings, an unexpected fracture following a minor fall, rapid loss of height, or back pain, or detection of thin bones on an X-ray done for some other reason.

A prudent lifestyle includes regular exercise (walking three times a week will do), a good intake of calcium and vitamin D as found in dairy products, or possibly by taking calcium (at least 1.5g a day) and vitamin D tablets if such a diet conflicts with other health problems such as raised cholesterol. People with significant osteoporosis can take medication such as alendronate. In future osteoporosis will probably be more aggressively identified and treated in recognition of increasing life expectancy and the fact that fractures due to osteoporosis are a major cause of disability in old age.

Prostate cancer

Many men now wish to be screened for this common cancer, but medical opinion is still divided on how to do so most reliably. There is a blood test – Prostate Specific Antigen or PSA- which gives an indication of early abnormalities in the prostate gland. This test can be taken together with a rectal examination of the prostate gland, the doctor feeling for hard nodules and irregularities within the gland. Unfortunately, a normal PSA and examination do not exclude cancer. A slightly raised PSA is not diagnostic of cancer but raises anxiety and might call for a biopsy of the gland to be sure, which in itself is unpleasant and carries health risks. Therefore opinion is divided on the value of all this as a screening procedure; many specialists advise reserving these tests for men who are experiencing symptoms such as difficulty in passing urine. Hopefully this controversy will be resolved in the next few years, as more reliable blood tests become available.

Bowel cancer

Another controversial area, with current research looking at means of screening for this common malignancy. There is no agreed process at present.

Cancers of breast, womb, ovary and cervix

In general, the probability of all these cancers increases with age but there is no proven screening process other than self-awareness. Mammography is offered in the UK from the age of 50; routine cervical cancer screening stops at the age of 60. There are no tests for cancer of the womb or ovaries, despite much research into possible screening blood tests. Speak to your doctor or nurse about learning how to examine your breasts – this is a sensitive method of detecting early breast problems. Otherwise it is a matter of being aware of warning symptoms (of which more below).

Checks on heart and lungs

Just occasionally a doctor may pick up an abnormality on examination of which you were unaware. In the heart this is most likely to be an irregular heart rhythm. The commonest is atrial fibrillation, where the heart beats in a rapid, unco-ordinated way; this often causes no symptoms other than feeling palpitations but it can affect breathing. Another common rhythm is to drop beats, or heart block, where the heart beats extremely slowly. Chances are, however, that you would have already been aware of a problem in these cases. Finding an unsuspected lung abnormality is even more unlikely in the absence of breathing difficulties, cough or breathlessness.

As you get older

It is still worth having the checks already mentioned. In addition there are lifestyle checks worth remembering. These relate to personal safety; for example:

- Is your home safe?
- Is wiring sound?
- Are carpets and rugs firmly fitting?
- Are there unnecessary trailing flexes?
- Is the lighting good?
- Are your gas and electrical supplies safe and the appliances that use them?
- Can you get safely into and out of the bath and shower?
- Should you have grab handles?
- Are steps to your door accessible and non-slip?
- Do you have warm clothing and an emergency supply of food in case you get isolated for any reason?
- Can you summon emergency help?
- Are there people who will keep an eye out for you?

Vaccinations

It is easy to overlook the need to keep certain vaccinations up to date. One often forgotten is tetanus; have a booster every 10 years; this is especially important if you are a gardener with an increased hazard of contracting tetanus through cuts contaminated with soil. Consider an annual flu vaccination; this really is advisable if you have diabetes, chronic chest disease, heart trouble or any illness that reduces your immunity, such as certain blood conditions. Flu vaccination needs to be given every year, because the nature of the flu virus varies from year to year. Vaccination reduces the risk of catching flu by about 80 per cent; this means true flu, not colds. People in the higher risk categories should also consider having vaccination against pneumococcus, a bacteria that can cause serious chest infections and pneumonia. This is a vaccination that is only needed once, except for certain unusually susceptible individuals who might need it every few years – your doctor can advise you further.

So why have check-ups at all?

A good question. Many doctors feel they are a waste of time, other than the basic checks on blood pressure and for diabetes. On the other hand, individuals find them reassuring, even though there is a low probability of revealing something of which you were not already aware.

How to help yourself: Simple remedies for simple problems

Joint pains

These are the aches and pains to be expected as you get older; joints commonly affected are the hips, knees, thumbs, neck and shoulders. Pains due to wear and tear are often worse after a period of rest such as on waking in the morning, but improve as the day goes by and are helped by warmth and relieved by resting the joint. Consider whether you need a painkiller at all; perhaps a warm bath will do, or resting. If only a couple of easily accessible joints are affected, try an embrocating cream first such as ibuprofen gel. Many are available over the counter, stronger ones are on prescription.

Use a painkiller only if essential and start with the simplest and cheapest that works for you – typically paracetamol with or without a small quantity of codeine, or ibuprofen tablets. These are generally well tolerated and go with most other medication you may be on. Check with the pharmacist or doctor if you are on medication for asthma, chronic airways disease, or indigestion or have liver or kidney problems.

Warning signs and symptoms

- A single hot swollen joint
- Redness over a painful joint or muscles
- Pain after trauma
- Pain in the night
- Pain not relieved by simple measures
- Generalised joint pains, especially flitting from joint to joint.

Colds, coughs and sore throats (upper respiratory infections)

The older you are the more immunity you build up to the many viruses that cause these problems; therefore they are less common in older people than children. They begin typically with tickling in the throat, shivers and feeling off colour. You are less likely than children to have a high temperature. After a few days your nose runs, your ears feel muffled and you have a cough, often with some coloured sputum. The whole picture settles down over a few more days, lasting 7–10 days in all. Commonly a cough persists for a couple of weeks longer.

As self-help take paracetamol for temperatures, aches and pains; drink 50 per cent more fluid than you normally would and do not worry about not eating for a few days. You will feel more comfortable by staying in an even temperature. Also helpful are throat sprays to relieve pain and decongestant sweets to relieve blockages. Cough mixtures are soothing; choose the cheapest and best tasting that helps you. Prop up your pillows so that you sleep more upright and keep your bedroom at an even temperature overnight to reduce coughing (but it does not need to be hot). These simple measures will relieve most such illnesses; antibiotics are normally of no value; they will neither relieve symptoms nor shorten the illness (but see also below).

Warning signs

- High temperatures persisting more than 3–4 days
- Increasingly productive cough
- Breathlessness
- Inability to drink
- Unusual weakness

- Confusion
- Chest pains.

These symptoms suggest a more deep-seated bacterial infection on the lungs which affects your body more severely. See your doctor; you may need an antibiotic in such circumstances, or even hospital admission depending on your overall state of health and support at home. You should also be cautious if you have other illnesses which makes you more susceptible to the effects of infections. Most commonly these would be diabetes, heart disease, chronic lung disease such as chronic bronchitis. In these circumstances most doctors will readily prescribe an antibiotic in the hope of stopping the illness from affecting your lungs more severely.

Indigestion

The symptoms are a burning sensation in the gullet or the upper abdomen after eating, often with acid rising into the mouth. The symptoms are made worse by acidic or highly spiced foods, worry, smoking and alcohol consumption. These are incredibly common symptoms, as witnessed by the great numbers of remedies available over the counter. Self-help includes taking an antacid remedy; choose one with aluminium hydroxide for best effect, as those made with magnesium can cause diarrhoea. Choose one with antiflatuent foam; these tend to be more effective for indigestion in the gullet and at night. Reduce smoking and alcohol consumption and avoid tight clothing, which increases abdominal pressure and the reflux of acid from the stomach into the gullet. Eat small, regular meals rather than large and distending meals. Chronic sufferers should sleep with the head of the bed raised and avoid the highly spiced foods and indigestible or pickled foods that commonly provoke indigestion. Check your teeth; are they preventing you chewing food properly?

If these remedies fail or are inadequate, seek your doctor's advice. There are many powerful acid-reducing medications that relieve severe indigestion for most people. Also your doctor will consider the need for further investigation to determine the cause, which could be a chronic ulcer, hiatus hernia, or cancer of the stomach or gullet.

Warning symptoms

- Indigestion new for you in its persistence or severity
- Vomiting blood
- Passing black motions (a feature of internal blood loss)
- Weight loss and loss of appetite
- Difficulty swallowing food or fluids
- Indigestion pain radiating into your back
- 'Indigestion pain' made worse by exertion – this could be angina instead
- Chest pain over your gullet new for you and persisting more than a few minutes – this could again be heart pain.

See your doctor in these circumstances; they will want further investigations and checks.

Constipation

This refers to difficulty in opening your bowels, generally through hardness of the motions or pain. Though periods of constipation happen at all ages, it gets more common with age for reasons that include less fluid intake, taking drugs which constipate (especially painkillers containing codeine or similar), and poorer mobility (because being mobile stimulates the bowel).

Self-help: firstly, be sure you know what you mean by constipation. It is unnecessary to have a movement every day; everyone has their own usual pattern, which can vary from bowels open three times a day to twice a week. It is normal for the hardness or frequency of motions to vary from day to day and week to week, reflecting your diet, food intake and mobility. Do not rush straight to laxatives for each small variation.

Next, laxatives. There are two broad groups:

- Those which increase the bulk of the motions, making them easier to pass; examples are fibre drinks, cellulose bulking agents, lactulose and bran. These are to be preferred because they work with your body, keep the intestines functioning and reduce the effort needed to open your bowels.
- Then there are those laxatives which stimulate the bowel to pass a motion, including senna and phenophthalein. These have a role

if the bowel has become lax and lazy, which generally happens in advanced old age, especially where you need to take drugs which constipate – typically, powerful pain killers. Such laxatives may cause abdominal cramps, through stimulating muscle action, and diarrhoea; also the bowel comes to rely on them, so you find that they become a constant necessity.

Drink more fluids: 1–2 litres a day is a normal intake; increase this by 50 per cent to 2–3 litres day. Select foods which are naturally high in fibre such as vegetables, bran-enriched cereals and bread, brown rice, apples. If your body tells you to open your bowels, obey! There is a reflex to do so after eating that is similar to a baby filling its nappy soon after feeding. Heed the call. Medical options include higher doses of laxatives, more stimulant laxatives and, rarely, suppositories or enemas to clear out particularly stubborn problems.

Warning signs
These include:

- Constipation new for you, with no obvious cause and lasting more than a couple of weeks
- Bleeding from the back passage or blood on the motions
- Abdominal pain.

These can point to growths within the rectum or large intestine and you should see a doctor about this.

Poor sleep

Your need for sleep naturally decreases as you get older, so that 5–6 hours a night is perfectly normal for many people by their late 50s. Add the fact that you may be less active and doze in the day and it is easy to find that you sleep less at night. This is not insomnia but simply reflects that there is a limit to how much sleep you need in a day. Others find sleep is disturbed through discomfort, the need to pass water frequently, apprehension about sound, or your partner disturbing you. Perhaps your bed is uncomfortable, the temperature highly variable, or sounds and lights break into your consciousness. Do something about these factors before deciding that you have an actual sleep problem. Signs that there may indeed be a problem are increasing daytime drowsiness, inability to concentrate and irritability.

Self-help: judge how much sleep you need to feel comfortable; do not fritter this away with naps and snoozes during the day. Ensure that your bedroom is comfortable, the pillows as you wish, with an even temperature and shaded from noise and light. These are basic things but it is surprising how easy it is to overlook them. It is unnecessary to keep bedrooms warm; rather there should be an even temperature of, say, 60–65 degrees; it is changes in temperature that set off disturbances. Make a routine for going to bed – reading, taking a bath, making yourself comfortable. Avoid stimulant drinks such as tea and coffee for at least two hours before bed – some people find they must avoid them even longer. Try relaxation techniques such as concentrating on relaxing all your muscles, visualising a soothing scene and focusing on soothing thoughts. Try sex – it is a natural, time-tested way of going to sleep.

There are various natural remedies for sleep such as St John's Wort and calamine teas. Many people find that an alcoholic drink before bed helps sleep; choose one which does not cause other problems such as making you pass urine later in the night, or which leaves you feeling heavy headed the next morning.

Sleeping tablets should be regarded as a final resort where sleeplessness is having a serious effect on your activities during the day. Though modern sleeping tablets are safe, they do carry a potential for habituation, so that you find you need more to achieve an effect. You can become dependent on sleeping tablets within just a fortnight of regular use, in the sense of having several sleepless nights as a rebound if you miss taking them. Modern drugs include temazepam and zopiclone.

Warning signs
- Persistent insomnia
- Waking early in the morning and lying there in anxiety and apprehension.

These are classical features of depression.

Skin infections

Because the skin becomes more fragile as you get older, minor cuts and grazes are likely to take longer to heal; in addition the skin becomes less supple with age and more liable to crack and this in turn makes it easier for infection to enter the skin. For these reasons you should treat even minor cuts and abrasions carefully. Use one of the many over-the-counter antiseptic creams, with a light dressing to provide protection to the healing cut. However, leave the skin exposed whenever safe to do so. Cuts on the shin and feet are slower to heal than elsewhere, because the blood supply to those regions is naturally poor and tends to worsen with age, and there is therefore a risk of a cut turning into an ulcer. For this you may need medical and possibly nursing help to promote healing, with antibiotic creams or tablets and any of a range of dressings that promote healing and protect the healing skin.

Be careful when trimming your nails, making sure that you do not accidentally cut the skin, as that is an easy and common route for infection. People with diabetes and poor circulation to the feet should pay particular attention to nail care, as they are so much more prone to problems if infection gets in through poorly cut nails.

Warning signs
These include:

- Redness spreading around the wound (skin infection)
- Failure to heal after a few days
- Increasing pain
- A green/yellow discharge, often smelly.

Seek medical help in these circumstances. Be particularly fussy about injuries if you have diabetes or conditions that reduce the blood flow to your legs.

When to seek help – a summary of warning signs and symptoms

The leisure you enjoy as you get older gives you more time to be aware of your body and its small deviations from what you regard as 'normal'; it is easy, too easy, to become obsessed by every little symptom, each new pain or new sensation. Nevertheless there are certain symptoms that you should take seriously and consider seeking medical advice about. For the rest, you have to develop a sense of 'normal abnormality' otherwise you can become wracked by anxiety with each day's new sensation. The following are a range of important symptoms for which you should see a doctor. Often there will be an innocent explanation and a readily treated cause, but these can be early features of cancers, cardiovascular disease, hormone problems (especially diabetes) and psychiatric problems, including Alzheimer's disease.

Skin

- A sore which does not heal
- A coloured patch or mole which gets darker, itches, bleeds and looks irregular
- Persistent itching
- An ulcer
- Widespread spontaneous bruising (small bruises are very common).

Heart, lungs and circulation

- Unusual breathlessness
- Hoarseness lasting more than 2 weeks
- Pain/heaviness over the chest on exertion
- Chest pain
- Cough lasting more than 2-3 weeks
- Coughing blood
- Pains in the thighs/legs on walking
- Pains in the feet.

Digestive system and bowels

- Severe/persistent indigestion
- Difficulty swallowing food or drink
- Vomiting blood
- Persistent abdominal pain
- Abdominal swelling
- Diarrhoea/constipation lasting more than 2 weeks
- Blood from the rectum
- Black motions
- Mouth ulcers persisting more than 2 weeks.

Genito-urinary system

- Vaginal bleeding after the menopause, unless expected with HRT
- Blood in the urine
- Discharge from penis/vagina
- Swelling around the genitalia, including the testicles
- Difficulty passing urine.

Brain and nervous system

- Weakness/paralysis of a limb
- Persistent unusual numbness or sensations
- Slurred speech
- Rapidly deteriorating memory, comprehension.

Senses

- Blurred vision, rapid loss or distortion of vision
- Pain in the eyes
- Persistent dizziness
- Rapid loss/distortion of hearing.

Muscles/bone

- Persistent bone pain, including back pain
- Tender muscles.

Psychological

- Rapid change of personality, especially together with memory loss or confusion
- Depression, especially with suicidal thoughts; paranoia
- Unusual anxiety or irritability; self-neglect
- Alcoholism.

General

- Significant weight loss or weight gain
- Loss of appetite
- New lumps, swellings
- Unusual tiredness
- Persistent fever
- Unexpected bleeding from any part of the body.

Anxiety and depression

These are surprisingly common symptoms as you get older, often for easily understood reasons – losses through health and bereavement, worries about finances, partners and other family members. Perhaps your own children are going through difficulties which naturally concern you. Other causes are a little less rational: perhaps you deplore the state of the country, see a general decline and feel pessimistic about what the future holds. Perhaps you worry about personal safety when out or even in your home – a fear just not borne out by statistics, which show that it is the young who are far more often the targets of violence, robbery or muggings rather than the elderly. Perhaps retirement has not turned out as fulfilling as you hoped – maybe the new interests never materialised, you find it difficult to make new friends, you lack enthusiasm for starting afresh. Perhaps you realise that your working life was of such fundamental importance to you that it really is irreplaceable. These are serious concerns that can lead to chronic anxiety.

Symptoms of anxiety typically include a feeling of constantly being on edge, sweating, palpitations (awareness of heart rate), disturbed sleep, feeling tired all the time, neck pains and headaches from constant muscle tension, diarrhoea and a feeling that your memory and attention span have worsened. In an effort to relieve anxiety you may turn to alcohol, tobacco or other drugs. Friends and relatives notice that you are on edge, snappy, irritable and unable to settle to things. You have a constant sense of apprehension and worry.

Depression is an all-pervasive state which gradually saps life of most of its interest. Depression in later life is often precipitated by the inevitable losses of old age through disease, disability and death. Often, and understandably, people will review their life, their relationships and achievements and wonder what it was all about. Did they reach their potential, did they make mistakes, or was life just unfair? As human beings, our aspirations so often exceed our abilities; therefore, no matter how successful life has been, it is always possible to identify shortcomings and wrong turnings: things that you had rather not done and things – usually so many more – that you wish you had.

This is not unhealthy in itself, because it is important to your mental stability to come to some sort of accommodation and reconciliation with how your life has been. People differ greatly in their need for this; some of us never look back and never regret, others need to reassess and reassure themselves that they did their best.

Slowly and insidiously regret can turn to sadness, then to depression. Or depression may arise as a pure illness outside your ability to rebuff or influence, through some change in your brain chemistry still incompletely understood.

The symptoms of depression often overlap with those of anxiety. Indeed, depression in later life often seems initially more of an anxiety state than does depression at younger ages. Further features are sadness, crying, poor sleep, typically waking earlier than usual, loss of interest in food, sex and general activities. As depression deepens you may come to doubt the motives and goodwill of others in your life, become obsessed by the fear of physical illness despite reassurance and turn to drink. Eventually you think of suicide as a way out of the misery.

Treatment

Support

The support and understanding of family and friends is of immense importance in convincing you that you are a worthy person and in guiding you back to the person you once were. So talk to them about your anxieties and worries; you may be surprised to find how many of these they share. They will also help you to put things into perspective. This is not to explain away anxiety or sadness, the roots of which may be perfectly understandable. Rather, it is to break a cycle of emotion feeding on itself which any of us might experience, left to our own solitude and thought processes.

Explanation and reorganisation

There are many circumstances where worry or depression are to be expected, such as after bereavement or financial problems. Initially you need reassurance that your emotions are valid in these circumstances. But this is not enough; next you need constructive help to overcome the root cause. If it is a financial problem, you need help to work it out, re-budget, sell assets or otherwise rearrange your affairs. If the problem is bereavement, you need to be helped through a grieving process (see more below). If it is fear of illness, then a check-up that reassures you about your state of health should help. If worry, it can help to be shown how over-breathing or focusing on feared thoughts can provoke anxiety and palpitations. If you are fearful of personal safety, taking steps to improve home security, installing an alarm for when you go out and strategies for avoiding trouble can all reassure you.

Counselling

This is used in its broadest sense to include all sources of outside help that are not directly connected to you through friendship or family ties. It can range from financial advisers, police safety officers, housing advisers and insurance brokers through to bereavement counsellors and psychotherapeutic counsellors. A roofing contractor as a counsellor? Why not? If your fear is of your house leaking while you are out, it is therapeutic to have the advice of a skilled and trusted roofer to sort out what needs to be done.

What do these all have in common? They are trained to lead you through your situation and pick out the essential difficulties, goals and aspirations. They get you to consider things you might rather not think about – at one extreme death, inheritance tax, replacing loose tiles and fitting security lights; at the other, unresolved emotions from your own childhood, relationships with your family and children, your assessment of yourself. Only after you have honestly identified such factors can you start a constructive process of dealing with them.

Medication

There is still a puzzling stigma about medication for psychological problems. You would not tough out a chest infection or brazen your way through a broken leg. So why put up with crippling anxiety or depression? Probably an older generation thinks it is 'natural' to have such emotions and somehow a sign of weakness to take medication for them. To some degree this is not wrong; life is anxiety-provoking and frequently depressing and often there is absolutely nothing you can do about it. So how can you decide when your depression or anxiety has gone beyond the 'background level' inherent in life? The answer is, when it is interfering with your ability to function normally. This is something your friends or relatives may be more aware of than you, if you are becoming reclusive or always on edge, for example.

At this point a course of medication can be very helpful. Choices include mild sedatives such as valium, to take when on edge. Provided these are not taken regularly, they are not addictive and are safer than taking excessive alcohol. Next there are anti-depressants, of which there is an extensive choice. They include tricyclics (dothiepin, amitryptiline). These are sedating, which can be useful if poor sleep is part of the problem. They are toxic in overdose, so doctors may instead use one of the SSRIs, modern anti-depressants that are safe in overdose. These include Prozac (fluoxetine) and Seroxat (paroxetine). They are relatively free of side effects.

Alternative therapies

Consider relaxation classes, including yoga, meditation, massage and alternative herbal preparations. Exercise is a great stress-buster, whether it is walking, dancing, swimming, golf, or more formal training. And how about a pet?

Bereavement

The experience of loss through death is inevitable as you reach middle age, and increasingly so the longer you live. Initially you will lose people older than yourself, people in your parents' generation and your parents themselves. Comes a time when the people you lose are closer to your own age, though this will probably not be common until you are well into your 60s, if not later. A few people may have the tragedy of losing a child.

For many people the major effect of bereavement, apart from the sadness itself, is loss of support. This may be why widowers cope less well after bereavement than widows who are used to caring for themselves. Bereavement has an important effect on physical health, as shown by increases in mortality especially in the first year after bereavement, though again the effect is much less in widows than in widowers.

There are well recognised stages of grief which it can be a comfort to know are normal. Knowing this also helps you to measure when grief is in danger of becoming abnormal in its duration or depth. These stages are:

- Shock, the emotional blast of loss, grief, disorientation
- Denial, worrying whether a mistake caused the death
- Depression
- Guilt, turning on things left unsaid or undone and emotions not reconciled
- Anxiety about being alone and coping
- Anger from the circumstances of the death, the actions (or inactions) of others
- Resolution as emotions settle down and things get into perspective
- Renewal, moving on in life with new relationships and interests and setting the deceased person in context

How to cope with bereavement

Admit the loss
This may seem odd; how can you not admit a bereavement? But persistent anger or guilt actually prevent the loss from settling by keeping a hurt alive. Therefore you need an opportunity to confront these emotions. Just talking about the deceased is often enough.

Identify and ventilate feelings
You may need help in this, especially in acknowledging feelings of guilt, resentments and other uncomfortable emotions. It is best to release these at this stage or they will come back to haunt you at other times.

Explore life without the deceased
This should not make you guilty; if your relationship was a good one, this is what they themselves would want for you. Then there are practical aspects to be sorted out – whether to move house, finances, documents, etc.

Discourage emotional withdrawal
In other words, do not slide into isolation nor into a fear of emotional investment in other people.

Allow time
It can take a couple of years to adjust fully to a close bereavement. six to twelve months is not uncommon and in a sense bereavement never ends. Though it is a truism, time does heal.

Your feelings are normal
All the above stages are to be expected, as is the time-scale outlined.

Allow for differences
People grieve at different rates. It is not indifference to get on with life after two weeks, nor is it necessarily abnormal to still feel a loss keenly after three years, though it would be if it was at the cost of not taking up a normal life again.

Accept support

This is simply the opportunity to talk, reminisce, express emotions.

Allow for differences in coping

Different people cope in their own ways and this cannot always be predicted from their previous personality. The survivor of a couple apparently on cool terms may be far more affected than an apparently devoted couple; the reasons for this may lie in deep psychological undercurrents that were not apparent to an outsider, or be the result of faith, religious faith or philosophy.

Be prepared to seek medical help

At the initial shock, people may need medical help to cope with grief and give sleep. This should be kept to a minimum because there is no sense in drugging a natural reaction into oblivion – it will only return. At some point, usually after two or three months, you should be returning to a more normal pattern of activity, sleep and emotion, and be getting enjoyment out of life again. If this is not the case you may be slipping into a depression (see earlier). Here medication may be of value, not as a substitute for coming to terms with the bereavement, but as a means of getting things into perspective.

How to keep safe and feel secure

It is important as you get older to keep your environment as safe as you can, without going to extremes; you need to acknowledge changes in your speed of reaction, your balance and the possibility of confusion in some circumstances. Accidents are an important cause of disability once you reach 65 and beyond, and especially once you are in your 70s, when road accidents and falls are a major problem. How to avoid these calls for some streetwise precautions.

Physical safety

- Wear well-fitting shoes that do not slip in wet or icy conditions; better still, consider whether your bad weather journey is really necessary.

- Ensure that you have good lighting around the home and when out at night; this is all the more important in hazardous areas such as steps, garden paths and road crossings.
- Many older people rely on handles and rails for security when climbing stairs and getting into or out of a bath or shower.
- It is common sense to avoid any clutter in your home that increases the risk of tripping: clear away newspapers, don't have flexes trailing from appliances across areas where you walk, and secure rugs. This includes tidying away your grandchildren's toys.
- Be careful with open flames from candles and gas cookers, which you should not leave unattended. Consider having a fire extinguisher at home.

Personal safety and security

Many older people have a fear of being mugged or assaulted that is out of all proportion to the actual risk, which is very low. Do not let irrational fears turn you into a recluse; however, you should stick to the common-sense measures we all know – avoiding back streets and empty places at night, keeping to well-lit areas and walking away from circumstances where you feel apprehensive such as rowdy pubs and boisterous football crowds. You may feel more secure carrying a mobile phone or a personal alarm.

Probably more important is to keep your home secure and keep out strangers unless they have proof of identity. Fit a security chain and peephole so that you can see who is at the door; ask for official identification even from people from utilities like gas and electric. These and other responsible organisations can arrange to hold a password for your added security. Avoid dealing with unannounced door-to-door salesmen.

Get to know your neighbours, even if it is just by a nod in passing; that fleeting contact is enough to signal that you are all right and up and about. In that way they may get concerned if they fail to see you and will check that all is well; you could perhaps leave a key with a trusted neighbour, and it makes sense to carry contact numbers with you and keep them in a conspicuous place at home.

We all feel bewildered by the speed and complexity of life and this is likely to get worse. You may feel threatened by having to take quick decisions on complex issues that you do not fully understand, such as financial arrangements, quotations for services or contracts for equipment. Do not over-estimate the urgency of the decision; on the whole, time is more on your side than it is for a younger person still at work who has to take all these decisions but has less time to do so. Ask for time to consider; go over things until you understand them; and if you are still unsure ask the opinion of a trusted relative, friend or professional adviser. Try not to get into situations where things become urgent: for example, check your car and home regularly for maintenance problems rather than wait until the roof leaks; plan holidays in good time; and make a point of reviewing your personal arrangements, finances and legal situation regularly.

This is not meant to depress you into a state of paranoid insecurity; rather, the idea is to enhance your sense of safety and encourage you to go out, do things and purchase services. You can remain in charge and cope with complexity by planning and anticipating.

9

How to Keep an Active Mind: Memory, Learning and Understanding

Thou hast great allies; thy friends are exultations, agonies, and love, and Man's unconquerable mind.

Wordsworth

There is an idea that at the point when you retire your intellect goes into free fall, dropping through the stratosphere at least as fast as your income also falls. Those proposing this myth have certain things in common, like hair, all their teeth and unwrinkled skin. You've guessed it; it's those people waiting to step into your shoes as soon as they have waved you out of the door. It is one of the more pervasive assumptions in our society that age loses and youth gains. I am going to show how false this is. You may like to know the conclusion now, which is that while you remain healthy and active, you will remain capable of doing everything you did when younger. It may take longer and you may not be as skilful, but you can still perform.

The physical changes in the brain due to ageing are relatively modest – even by your 80s you will still have about 97 per cent of all your neurones (the basic nerve cells that make up much of the brain). There are indeed detectable changes in memory but these really only show themselves from the late 60s onwards and do not necessarily become significant until your 80s. The much feared Alzheimer's disease is a case in point. At the age of 65 it affects only about 2 per cent of the population; even by the age of 80–85, 80 per cent of that population are unaffected. This is not to detract from the seriousness of the condition and the tremendous burden it imposes on individuals, their carers and society; rather, it puts things in perspective. After retirement most people's intellectual abilities remain reasonably stable for a couple of decades. That is worth re-reading: a couple of decades.

Along with this, studies and personal experience have shown what many of us suspected: older people often have a more integrated, consistent, philosophical and comfortable overall view of their life than many younger people. This is to be expected, if you think about it. By the time of retirement you have probably managed the most active and demanding part of your life; you have had your achievements, failures and disappointments socially, work-wise and personally. Your life has been a process of adaptation – not that you necessarily saw it as such; at the time it may have felt just a pain and a struggle. Nevertheless, and in retrospect, adaptation is what it has been.

By retirement, the majority of people have reached some sort of reconciliation with the way their life has gone. This is not to say that they felt complacent or resigned – that implies a negativity that this whole book is arguing against! There are still goals to identify, aims to achieve and abilities to nurture. And yet, and yet, the wisdom of experience tells you that there are certain things that will not now change, certain events whose outcome can no longer be influenced and to which you must either reconcile yourself or else live in a state of dissatisfaction.

This has been called 'eldering' as opposed to the term 'senescence'. Eldering implies growing into a role accepted and valued by society, whereby older people are acknowledged as repositories of wisdom, mature judgement, broad perspectives and other positive qualities unlikely to be found in younger people.

It's never too late

Research has not confirmed the popular view that the ability to memorise inevitably deteriorates, at least for basic procedures such as numbers, addresses, directions and tasks. Though there are changes with age, in general these are not closely linked to age until you reach the late 70s or early 80s, when they do become important. Similarly, research has shown that older people retain the ability to learn new material or skills, though they do take longer.

The major difference between memory in the old and the young concerns the ability to recall that newly acquired learning; it is not that you forget it, but that you forget that you know it! For most day to day activities this is of no great significance; it does become important when you are faced with complex tasks demanding the 'recall and processing' of large quantities of information. Also there is some loss of ability to categorise information quickly in a way that enhances rapid retrieval and review when needed.

Even so, the differences between people of similar age greatly outweigh the effects of age alone. Your memory abilities are more a function of you as an individual than simply a reflection of how old you are.

Nor is there some end point beyond which you are no longer capable of any learning. With the exception of people with Alzheimer's, you will retain an ability to learn throughout your life. How you use that ability is up to you and your circumstances.

Maximise your senses to maximise your mind

There are some simple but important ways to make the most of your mental abilities. Though your mind may remain keen, some abilities are inevitably declining, especially vision, hearing and stamina. Therefore it is only common sense to make the best of what you have.

- Get the best glasses you can. Discuss with your optician whether one pair of glasses will let you 'get by' for both close and distant work, or whether it would be much more efficient to keep two pairs, each of which does the job properly. Arrange any reading area for comfort, with a good chair, good lighting (often best achieved with a reading lamp), an adequate desk and a pleasant, warm environment. Perhaps your hearing is impaired? Rather than struggle to hear broadcasts or follow conversation and lectures, accept gracefully that you need a hearing aid.

- Recognise that your stamina is less than it once was; build more rests into your day than when you were younger, though just how much of a rest you need will vary greatly from person to person. Take frequent breaks from whatever task or hobby you are pursuing – generally, every hour makes sense; be guided by your own feelings of tiredness or lapses of concentration. Take this into account if applying for courses of further study or new physical pursuits; how much of a commitment do they demand? If it is a full day, do you get breaks?
- It makes sense to go for courses geared to older people rather than mixed classes with the very young. Remember too that quite apart from differences in speed and memory, their agenda will not be your agenda. You may be learning, say, computer programming as a purely intellectual exercise, whereas for a younger person it may be with a view to a job. They will be impatient to make progress, whereas you may be keen to understand each aspect thoroughly. This will not make for a comfortable learning environment. The same goes for sports and physical activities; it makes plain sense to seek out others of a similar age and level of fitness rather than to play above your ability, agility or stamina.
- On the other hand, do not underestimate your capabilities in, for example, bridge and other card games, literature, wood turning, current affairs, rambling, car maintenance, genealogy, local history, golf and many other areas. These are areas where age either makes little difference or where skill and maturity more than compensate for changes in memory and in stamina.

An active mind in an active body

There is good experimental evidence to support this saying. People who maintain a level of physical fitness really do appear to maintain an active mind. We don't know for sure how much is cause and effect and how much it is a case of active older people being more likely to be active mentally anyway. But research points a way you would be unwise to ignore. Staying physically active does appear to enhance mental agility; it makes people feel better about themselves and therefore more able to cope with pressures and enjoy greater stamina.

Keeping up interests: being leisurely, not leisured

The importance of this cannot be over-emphasised. You may look forward to retirement as offering a good rest after a pressured life, and indeed that may be tremendously enjoyable initially. But it hardly ever remains enjoyable to lead a life of total leisure; the novelty of the experience will inevitably pall. Six months is all it can take to move from 'This is the life!' to 'Is this the life?' There are several reasons for this.

If you are reading this book, you may have retired from a demanding job with its status, friendships, challenges and frustrations. No matter how irritating it may have been at the time, to lose it is to enter an enormous void that lacks stimulation and that regular sense of achievement which enhances your self-esteem. I have written elsewhere of the importance of having a structure to your day, which it is so easy to lose after retirement. Initially, the sense of freedom more than fills that void, but it is not an adequate solution for most people most of the time; after six months or so you should be giving serious thought to how to fill the rest of your retirement. Ideally, you can draw on those skills you used during your working lifetime, or the hobbies which already enthral you. What will you gain from this?

- Self-esteem
- Recognition by others
- Structure to your time
- Long-term aspirations
- Maintaining mental and physical agility
- Personal growth
- Getting out from under your partner's feet.

These are needs and aspirations that interests will immediately satisfy. Other gains are less obvious and may not apply to everyone, for example:

- Earning more money
- Creating another career
- Avoiding boredom

- Distraction from other worries
- Finding new relationships
- Relieving guilt

Setting challenges

This may sound just what you are glad to escape from; who needs yet more demands on their time? The difference is that you are now the one setting the agenda and in so doing you are meeting your own requirements as opposed to those of your boss, partners, fellow-workers or clients. The exact nature of the challenge is really up to you, but it should be something fairly readily achievable; this is not the time in life to engineer disappointment into your lifestyle. If you already have a hobby, you could aim for a further qualification, a further level of skill, or recognition from other hobbyists. Perhaps you are at a stage where someone might profit from your experiences and wisdom – you could consider writing a book or pamphlet, or teaching (see also below).

It is useful to put time-scales on things. Where do you want to be next month? Next season? Next year? What should you be doing now to ensure that you hit that goal then? What resources do you need in terms of money, travel, or time? Do you need to juggle things around? Do you need to tell anyone else or is this your thing alone? Can you do this alone or do you need a supervisor, tutor or co-conspirator?

This may sound too formalised for you; perhaps you already know where you are going and will organise your time on an *ad hoc*, as 'needs arise' basis. This is fine; the present scheme is aimed more at the individual who is already finding the charms of total leisure wearing thin but is not quite sure what to do about it.

Here is a way to analyse things:

- What skills did you use in your career?
- And in your hobbies?
- Which skills still interest you?
- What are your limitations of time, health, money, other commitments?
- What next?

Now you are in a position to draw up a list of possibilities.

The ideal pursuit might be something that interests you greatly and yet does not require much investment of resources. You may now realise that other things are unlikely to repay the effort you have to put into them for the satisfaction achieved. Can you do something about these or are they essential to your lifestyle?

Some options

Reading

If you are reading this, you will probably already know the value of the printed word; here is your entry into imagination, travel, emotion, biography, knowledge and opinion. Chances are that you have been a reader throughout your life; now in retirement you can pursue that as far as you wish. Broadly, your reading will fall into three categories:

- News and information (papers, opinion)
- Fact (often for hobbies or general interest)
- Fiction (for sheer pleasure and imagination).

You already know what you like to read and will carry on doing so. But how about doing the following?

- Taking a different newspaper once a week
- Taking a news magazine occasionally
- Researching a topic intensively, something you like or that intrigues you
- Keeping a list of books or authors for when you go to the library or bookshop
- Considering a reading group
- Trying the classical authors; they've lasted for a reason
- Trying the authors featured in book prizes and reviews
- You've seen the TV adaptation, now read the book . . .

Writing

I hope that you feel that your life has had interest and variety and that there are lessons to pass on; if so, why not put them in writing? Here are some tips:

Before starting
- Who are you writing for: yourself, family, public?
- Biography, fact, fiction?
- Do you intend to write a book, or just observations
- Consider a writing group
- Have a scheme, even if it is just a title and chapter headings
- Write a sentence or two that summarise your subject and goal, then keep that in mind.

During writing
- Write first; editing can wait
- Use a word processor
- Back up your material or else keep your dog away from it . . .
- If your text bores you, just imagine the effect on your reader . . .
- Opinion is free but facts are sacred – check and recheck.

After
- Be prepared to revise and to discard
- Less is usually more; be ruthless with your editing
- You cannot achieve perfection; stop when it's merely brilliant...

Recording memories

You may not feel you have a book in you, yet feel that you have important memories which deserve a wider audience. If you have ever wanted to know more about your own family, your parents' lives and where your family came from, then you can understand that your children and relatives might want to know the same about you. You may feel that this could be a morbid preoccupation, especially if your own life has been difficult, with a poor childhood and painful memories of family, war and conflict. Bear in mind that this is your story; you are this person who came through such experiences to where you are now. Whether your life has been one of achievement or regret, you have a story to tell that will interest others in ways you cannot imagine because you are too close to your subject to realise its fascination.

Just think how intriguing most of us find details about social history, even of just 50 years ago. Why did people eat what they did? Were motivations different then from now? How could anyone have imagined that that dress was attractive? These are what your family will want to know in time and if not your immediate children, then your grandchildren and their children. Local record offices and archives are also very keen to gather oral recollections from older residents.

The scope for recording memories has never been greater: writing, video, the Internet, voice recording and compact discs as well as photos and mementoes. Consider these possibilities:

- A brief biography of yourself and your family
- What it was like to grow up when you did
- Your working life
- Your family, for better or worse (you might like to put a time embargo on this!)
- A scrap-book of mementoes, travel, people
- Your philosophy of life
- The best bits
- The worst bits
- Your hopes for the future.

Reminiscence groups

As they get older many people feel a sense of estrangement from society; this has perhaps never been as strong as it was in the last century, when the pace of change was so bewilderingly fast. It can be a comfort to pass time with people of your own generation and possibly your own background, who understand each other without the need to keep explaining. As a purely natural process you will be passing time with people of similar age, but you might not have considered actually talking over old times, new times and how you feel about things. This is not to everyone's taste; some may find it repellent or uncomfortable to dwell on the past; others already associate with people of shared background – at company social clubs, trade or professional associations, or as regulars at the same pub!

What can you get from these groups, apart from nostalgia? You will find that they trigger memories and these are as likely to be of good, funny and rewarding things as they are of irritating things, which the mind has mechanisms to repress. There will be shared strategies for coping with change or with the effects of the more uncomfortable memories. You may have a goal for your reminiscences – recording the history of an organisation or your locality, or what you all did during the flower power era.

Reminiscence groups have particular appeal to people in advanced old age, especially if your physical abilities become weaker so that you have less scope for other activities.

Teaching and talking

Here is another opening that draws on those skills you acquired from your work or hobbies. You may never have imagined that you have the expertise necessary to teach, but you may be underestimating yourself. After a lifetime of playing golf or designing circuits, bookkeeping or organising voluntary groups, yours is a surprisingly extensive store of knowledge. Opportunities to teach are mainly through colleges of further education or local community education, in day classes or evening classes. Some large organisations like to keep in touch with ex-employees as a resource to introduce to new recruits. Do some research in the locality or among your trade organisations; the stimulation from teaching is enormous and deeply satisfying, all the more because you do not have to do it as a living and so you can decide on how much pressure to accept. You may also find that groups such as the Women's Institute, Townswomen's Guild or the local history society are interested in hearing you talk about your memories or an unusual hobby.

Computers

Here is a secret the young would rather not acknowledge; the elderly have taken to computers and the Internet in a big, big way. With friendly software, easily accessible browsers and integrated computers, there are fewer and fewer barriers to making friends with computer technology and the Internet. It just takes time; anyone who has used computers knows just how time-hungry the learning process is and here is where older people have an in-built advantage. You may feel apprehensive about the technology; forget it. Computers are easy; how hard you make them is just up to you.

What they offer
- Enormous resources for research
- Great browsability into areas you might never have considered
- International contacts at a fraction of phone/post costs
- Cheapness
- An indoor activity in case of poor weather or disability
- Keeping in touch with minimal effort.

Disadvantages
- Phone bills mount up
- It is a solitary hobby
- It becomes addictive.

The benefits greatly outweigh the potential problems, so long as you keep limits on what you are doing.

Learning about computers and the Internet is straightforward. Teaching yourself is not hard, though a good manual helps. Most colleges run courses introducing computers, which will get you up to speed within weeks. And do not overlook the valuable resource of your own children and grandchildren who (once they have got over their surprise) are sure to be pleased to introduce you to the Web.

Games and mental activity

Anything which requires you to remember, analyse and plan will maintain your mental ability; if you can combine it with exercise, so much the better. Common, popular options are card games (especially bridge for its sociability), pub quizzes, chess, crosswords and rambling groups. The more active can consider bowls, tennis, badminton, golf or swimming groups. The list goes on. You may be put off at the thought of acquiring a new skill after retirement if it also involves meeting new people and joining existing groups. This is a natural worry, but not one that should preoccupy you too much. It is a fact of life that groups for older people are always in need of new blood, because of an inevitable turnover of membership. However, reduce your awkwardness by finding a friend to go with you or someone to introduce you into the group.

There are also mind games that you might overlook; these are simple exercises or attitudes to incorporate into your everyday life, just simple ways of keeping the brain in action – the mental equivalent of taking a daily walk.

- Make a mental review of what you plan to do each day – by all means write it down too.
- Take a couple of moments to recall what you did yesterday. Were there any tasks to carry over? Who did you see, where did you go?
- Every day read a paper, listen to the radio or watch the news – anything to keep oriented.
- Do you have plans for the rest of the week? Have you written them down?
- Do a daily crossword puzzle, word game, or quiz; every paper has them.
- Read and write something every day.
- Use people's names when you see them; say 'Hello Jane', not just 'hello'.
- Faced with figures, add them up mentally first (then cheat!).
- Before you ask someone to get something, try to remember for yourself where you put it.

Hardly rocket science, yet easy ways of maintaining mental tone – and useful too.

Committees

How I hesitate to suggest this! Does it conjure up a vision of boring groups pondering obscure regulations in draughty halls? Well, those you should avoid; but there are bound to be other worthwhile causes to which you could devote time. You will almost certainly have causes dear to your heart and everyone can make a contribution to organisations; you just need the motivation. Typical areas are:

- Local amenities
- Religious organisations
- Social/sports clubs
- Welfare groups
- Meals on wheels
- Voluntary help to the disabled (driving, visiting, hospital visitor)
- Political parties
- Charities
- Neighbourhood Watch schemes
- Magistrate.

Your area of expertise could be:

- Organising
- Bookkeeping
- Driving
- Selling
- Analysing
- Typing/secretarial
- Knowledge
- Repairs and maintenance.

Many people are put off by committee work but there is usually scope to decide just how involved you want to be and limit your involvement by standing for a specified period only. It is best to judge a committee by attending some meetings, talking to existing members and generally getting the flavour of the group. You will not want unreasonable demands, friction or financial claims, though these have to be balanced against social opportunities, a feeling of doing a worthwhile job and occupying your time. Your local library and local paper are good places to explore the range of committees in your area or you may already have contact with a local community centre or sports club and want to get more involved.

In summary

The way you passed time before retirement will be a good indicator of the way things will be after retirement. You are unlikely to discover a completely new mental attitude and personality. But this does not condemn you to continuing into old age in an unchanging way. If you have the will – and only you can produce that – you can find ways to stimulate your mind and meet new people with new experiences. You can to some extent overthrow your previous personality in certain circumstances. It helps to think of yourself as a different personality when you try something new; a role model may help, someone whose reactions and actions you could take as a guide to behaviour. Don't take this too far; at some point you have to reveal the real you; use it until you feel comfortable with your new life and mental agility.

Questions and answers

Q: I keep forgetting names. Am I going mad?   A: Almost certainly not; everyone has this difficulty; it's sometimes called benign forgetfulness and need not worry you as long as you have no difficulty recalling them at most times.

Q: What if I do forget lots of things and get confused?   A: There may be a problem here. Formal tests of memory and personality may be advisable – see your doctor.

Q: Is the cause of confusion always Alzheimer's?   A: By no means; doctors need to consider causes such as depression, an under-active thyroid gland, physical illnesses such as anaemia which can cause confusion, strokes and the effects of medication.

Q: I've never had any interests outside work and don't like people. What can I do.   A: Either change or reconcile yourself to a lonely, unfulfilled retirement. Try new things in very small doses and social gatherings that do not force you into conversation or activities. Then build from there.

10

Love, Sex and Grooming: Sex and Affection in Older Life

I was adored once too.

Shakespeare, *Twelfth Night*

Sexual function in men and women

Until surprisingly recently sexual activity was thought to end at about 50, or slightly later in cases of strength. This was based on no evidence at all – just sheer prejudice mingled with a certain uneasiness that sex should be conducted by people old enough to be your parents, including your parents. Why, that means that politicians are doing it, accountants, advertising executives and pensioners. Surveys from the 1980s onwards confirmed what probably people already knew: that sexual desire continues well into old age in both men and women and that sexual activity is the norm rather than a smutty aberration. That there are changes with age is undeniable but these are more to do with stamina and the mechanics of sex than sexual interest.

In youth, physical ability and libido meet in a happy accord of desire and stamina so that sex is common many times a week or even several times a day. Desire can set the pace, knowing that ability will cope; it is normal for new relationships to be marked by frequent and urgent sex which is central to the partnership. As time passes and as familiarity grows, sexual activity generally diminishes in frequency and intensity. There are great variations on this; for some couples daily intercourse may be the norm, diminishing over time to once or twice a week. Yet that level of activity might seem excessive to others who perhaps began at once or twice a week and fell back to once or twice a month or less.

Libido

Sexual desire is a quality more difficult to gauge than voting intentions; surveys suggest that male libido remains high throughout life and certainly into the 80s. The data about women's libido is less clear, no doubt partly reflecting that it is still culturally unacceptable for older women to acknowledge sexuality, even though on the surface ours is becoming a sexually open society. Such evidence as there is suggests that many women not only maintain sexual interest beyond the menopause but also find that their libido increases.

Whether this lasts throughout life as with men is harder to know, but the general view is that for many women it persists into the 60s. Any observer in an old age home hearing women bantering about sex will suspect that sexual interest persists at least into the 70s and 80s. Whether this is translated into sexual activity is less certain, it may be a case of 'I would if I could' or 'You mustn't so don't'.

Isolation, confinement to one's own home or an institution, lack of opportunity to make new acquaintances, shyness about sexual attraction: all these conspire to deny older people the expression of their sexuality. For these reasons it is likely that sexual frustration is a significant feature of the experience of life as you get older.

Does sex matter to you?

You may feel guilty or worried about reading more of this chapter. Ask yourself a few questions

- Sex: do you want it?

168

- Sex: does your partner want it?
- Have you discussed things with your partner?
- Is your aim sexual intercourse or to express affection?

These questions will help focus your reading of the rest of this chapter. There is no point in reproaching yourself for supposed lack of desire or performance if this is unimportant within your overall relationship. Equally, it does your partner a disservice and jeopardises your relationship if you take no heed of each other's interest in and desire for sex.

So the rule is that there are no rules, nor can frequency of sexual contact be taken as any real measure of the depth or feeling of a relationship; it is not like taking the temperature of a couple's relationship.

Old sex is different sex

If sex is not simply measured by frequency of intercourse, how is it to be assessed? Really by extending the definition of sex into a wider expression of love and affection, where the physical expression of sex is less crucial. Sex and affection show themselves in a different way – in compliments, cuddles and periods of time without conversation. This may not be sex in all its juicy glory but it is affection of a deep order, though the pleasures may seem obscure to others until they experience it.

Older sex allows different times of day; your schedule does not limit you to nights and weekends: you can chose to watch the midday news or go to bed instead. Children are no longer around to interrupt or demand attention and you need no longer worry about a lie-in when you feel like it. The risk of pregnancy has gone and though that can be a matter of regret, more often it is a great relief, especially since you can abandon the chemical or mechanical contraception you needed previously. Many people find this makes their love-making more liberated.

Your periods have finished, which releases that extra week per month for love-making (very few people continue intercourse during the menstrual cycle for both aesthetic and religious reasons). With freedom from periods goes freedom from premenstrual tension, which blights another week each month for many women and puts an unconscious pressure to 'get it right' on the two weeks that are clear in each cycle.

Women: changes with age

The mechanics are quite well understood and do not really change with age; engorgement of the genital region during arousal and rhythmic contractions of the womb and pelvic organs during orgasm, leading to a relatively brief relaxation after which women may be content to begin sex again. The areas providing sexual stimulation extend away from the groin to include breasts, nipples, lips and inner thighs as well as the generally sensuous effects of skin contact.

Lack of lubrication

Glands line the walls of the vagina and secrete a natural lubricant. That secretion increases during sexual arousal and allows more comfortable intercourse. It is common to find that lubrication decreases in the run up to the menopause and especially thereafter. The walls of the vagina become thinner and less able to take the trauma of normal intercourse, so that older women often experience pain on intercourse and soreness afterwards. This may extend to bleeding (but see later).

Arthritis

Stiffness of joints, painful muscles and backache all limit how easily you can find a comfortable position for love-making and may cause pain during intercourse itself, detracting from the pleasure of the experience.

Men: changes with age

There is a natural increase in how long it takes to recover after orgasm; in young men this can be just half an hour, by middle age it is more likely to be several hours. By the 70s and 80s it is likely to be a day or so; there are great natural variations in this. There is a tendency to take longer to achieve full arousal and erection and longer to go from stimulation to orgasm. This can be counted as advantage because it reduces the occurrence of premature ejaculation, a slightly woolly expression which means reaching orgasm before your partner has reached her sexual climax or before she has reached a level of lubrication that allows comfortable intercourse.

Impotence in men

There is uncertainty about the incidence of impotence as men get older. First a word about definitions. Impotence has a strict medical meaning: inability to achieve erection of the penis sufficient for satisfactory intercourse. If that is the goal for you and your partner, then clearly impotence is a major problem. However, it may be that penetrative sex is not your style at all. Perhaps you simply give each other pleasure, not even necessarily to the point of penetration and orgasm. In which case 'impotence' as so defined is less of a practical issue and more of a psychological problem – which is not really a problem at all except through your own expectations of sexual ability and performance.

If you cannot get or maintain a satisfactory erection, what needs to be done? The first thing is to consider medical reasons for impotence. These include the following:

Depression

Symptoms of depression are constant sadness, crying and disturbed sleep, especially waking early in the morning. There may be great anxiety and you may have experienced saddening events that triggered the depression, such as death and illness in loved ones.

Diabetes

This common problem affects a high percentage of over-60s and should be considered in all cases of impotence. The symptoms are thirst, weight loss, the need to pass large quantities of urine, including at night, plus a general sense of lack of well-being. Testing urine for sugar and a blood test of blood sugar make the diagnosis. Diabetes is a very important diagnosis in its own right, quite apart from impotence, which is really a side effect. Unfortunately, impotence may not respond to control of the diabetes, though good control can help. You may need to consider some of the artificial aids for impotence mentioned later.

Effects of medication

Many drugs affect potency as a side effect; this is easily overlooked. This includes some of the most widely used drugs for blood pressure control, such as bendrofluazide and atenolol. Also – and this does pose problems – some of the modern anti-depressants affect sexual function in both men and women. These are the SSRIs which include fluoxetine (Prozac), but also older anti-depressants such as amitryptiline. These effects have to be balanced against the reason for taking the anti-depressant and this is something to discuss with your doctor. Be reassured that sexual function will return when you stop taking the medication.

Alcohol excess

This is another cause that is surprisingly easy to overlook when high alcohol consumption may be an important part of your post-retirement lifestyle. Perhaps unconsciously, your consumption has escalated from a drink most days to several drinks a day, a constant round of starters, accompaniments, finishers and sundowners. Monitor your intake in terms of units per week, where a unit is one glass of wine, one measure of spirits or half a pint of beer. Recommended maximums for men are 28 units, for women 21. Be aware that individuals respond in different ways, so that alcohol may have a role in impotence when your consumption is within those limits but has risen significantly compared with your usual intake.

Alcoholism itself may be recognised by a craving for alcohol, drinking in the morning and neglecting your health and home to pay for alcohol. Additional signs, apart from impotence, are tremor, high blood pressure and indigestion. Blood tests might reveal liver damage. You need to take yourself in hand as soon as possible, especially if your drinking is in response to post-retirement isolation, loneliness or depression.

Neurological problems

These include the after-effects of strokes, damage to the base of the spine through trauma, the effects of abdominal surgery for conditions such as bowel tumours and the after-effects of prostate surgery. Various rare neurological conditions such as multiple sclerosis can also cause impotence problems, but impotence alone is most unlikely to be the first symptom of a hitherto undiagnosed neurological problem.

Blood flow problems

Narrowed arteries are common in later life and where these involve the arteries supplying blood to the penis, impotence can result. The diagnosis is not too difficult if there are other symptoms of poor blood flow to the lower body, such as pains in the legs on exercising (termed claudication).

Psychological or physical?

This can be difficult to disentangle and probably most cases are a mixture of the two, where past failure leads to worry about future performance. There is probably a psychological cause if you still wake with an erection, get wet dreams and find that you get an erection with a certain partner and not with another. Physical causes are more likely if you never get a satisfactory erection. That said, impotence that is new for you should trigger a visit to the doctor for some basic physical checks.

What can be done?

Don't panic; impotence is common, often temporary and often treatable. A couple of episodes may require nothing more than trying again with a sympathetic partner in relaxed surroundings, without an unspoken urgency to 'perform'. Beyond that the choice ranges from mechanical appliances to medication. Medication now offers self-injection into the penis of a drug (alprostadil) that stimulates blood flow to the penis. This is quite an effective method which is well tolerated but calls for a degree of premeditation that in itself is off-putting, while some men simply cannot cope with giving themselves an injection.

Current breakthroughs are with the drug sildenafil (Viagra) and with MUSE. Sildenafil is the first of what will be a crowded class of drugs that induce erection through effects on a nerve transmitter called nitrous oxide. It works well in a high percentage of men, with headache as the main side effect. It is unsafe for men with heart trouble or angina. In the UK it is available on prescription to men with certain definite medical conditions such as diabetes, but is otherwise restricted to private sale.

MUSE is a pellet inserted into the tip of the penis, which appeals to men who do not wish to take a tablet or self-inject; the drug is exactly the same as that used in injections (alprostadil). Side effects are infrequent but it must not be used by men with deformity of the penis and certain other restrictions which your doctor will explain.

These methods are suitable for men with intact nerves and blood flow; difficulties arise for men with problems in those systems who may have to look for artificial mechanical devices. It is possible to implant inflatable tubes into the penis, pumping these up when desired; this sounds bizarre but modern devices are quite discreet.

Arthritis, operations and illness

These are more likely to affect the man if he is taking the initiative in sexual activity – he will be the one moving and exerting himself and so he may be more aware than his partner of the effects of stiff joints and breathlessness during intercourse, even the discomfort of angina in extreme moments. Being the odd organisms that men are, it is common for fear of symptoms to feed back through the psyche and induce impotence. Before long you are in a vicious cycle.

More of a problem might be the effects of certain operations on yourself or your partner such as hysterectomy and colostomy. The basis for these worries is often more apparent than real; you might have to experiment with positions and depth of penetration, empty your bladder and bag before sexual activity and avoid drinks for several hours beforehand. If you are on medication to control incontinence it helps to take it before sex to ensure maximum effect. And remember that familiarity breeds contentment. It is natural to feel upset at the new operation scar and the new device when first home from hospital, but if your relationship is a loving one any embarrassment will soon lessen.

Sexual problems and impotence in women

Orgasm and arousal

Impotence is not a term used as much with women as with men; you may hear the phrase 'orgasmic dysfunction' for women unable to achieve orgasm. This begs the question of the importance of orgasm for women, a highly controversial area. Many women have no particular need to achieve orgasm in order to have a sex life which they regard as satisfactory; this is a reflection of the wider scope of sexuality in women, which includes stimulation of the whole body within a caring, affectionate relationship. Achieving orgasm each time or even regularly is less important than the security of the expression of affection and the context in which sex takes place. In other words, sex for women is generally less goal-oriented than it is in men.

That said, there are plenty of women for whom orgasm is important, perhaps not each time but certainly at some times during a relationship. Surveys, as far as they can be relied upon, also show that only a minority of women achieve orgasm during intercourse; many require additional stimulation to do so before coitus. Older men should bear this in mind, if they haven't already learned it through their own experience; methods include manual stimulation of the clitoris, oral stimulation and using mechanical aids such as vibrators.

This may seem off-putting for an older couple for whom sex and its mechanics are likely to have been a more closed topic than for younger people. Nevertheless it is something to deal with if sex is becoming an issue between you and your partner, you are feeling unfulfilled sexually and your partner seems to need guidance on how to achieve satisfaction for you as well as for himself. Ironically, older people may need to be more open and explicit about their requirements than younger people who can take it for granted that 'the apparatus' will work.

Medication and hormone replacement therapy

Women also need to be aware that drugs can affect their libido and ability to climax; as with men the commonest drugs to do so are anti-depressants such as fluoxetine (Prozac), where the psychological benefits need to be balanced against these physical disadvantages. On the horizon is 'Viagra for women' – sildenafil tailored to heighten women's sexual response. At the time of writing it is unclear whether this will allow women to become orgasmic or intensify the experience.

Post-menopausal changes often make sex uncomfortable through dryness of the vagina. The simplest treatment is to use a lubricating gel such as KY jelly; these are safe and non-irritant and unlikely to result in allergies either for the woman or the man. A more physiological cure is with a gel containing female hormone, most often oestrogen, applied directly into the vagina. Over a few weeks this restores the walls of the vagina to a pre-menopausal state, moister, thicker and more resistant to the trauma of intercourse.

Then there is hormone replacement therapy, available now in a great array of forms – patches, tablets, gels and implants; your doctor will guide you towards a form suitable for you. HRT restores vaginal health and provides other worthwhile benefits such as reducing the rate of osteoporosis, helping joints feel more supple and relieving the aches and pains so common after the menopause. Most women can take HRT, the main exceptions being women with breast cancer or a strong family history of breast cancer or with previous blood clotting problems. You need regular monitoring of side effects and blood pressure but HRT is a generally safe and effective form of therapy, certainly for 5–8 years, though there are still uncertainties about its safety beyond that length of time. It can even be taken by women with heart trouble or high blood pressure, though medical opinion about this does have a tendency to change regularly.

Some specialists see no reason to stop HRT at all, even into your 70s; this is still an extreme view but one likely to become more accepted with an older population.

The mechanics of sex

Stiff joints, bad backs, inflexible hips, dicky hearts, breathlessness on exertion, incontinence. Oh dear, so many barriers to sex, you may think. Not so; where there is a desire there is a way, but it does take openness, discussion and shedding of embarrassment. Presumably you would not have read to this point if sex was unimportant to you. If it is unimportant, stop reading now. You who are still here need to accept that the physical changes that make sex less than pleasurable can nearly always be overcome with mutual consent and ingenuity. If your problem is joint pain and stiffness, try a change of position from the traditional 'missionary' male on female to side by side or entering from the rear. Experiment with placing pillows to raise your hips, to support an uncomfortable back. Ensure you empty your bowels and bladder before sex; avoiding direct pressure on the abdomen will reduce the chance of leaks.

Getting breathless? Take a rest, this is not a race; equally, the risks of a heart attack during sexual activity are greatly exaggerated, possibly through a desire to see this as the ideal way to quit this life. You do need to be aware of your body, adjusting your activity to the amount that your body can cope with in comfort. Stop if you experience chest pain or get too breathless. As long as you are sensible, you can discard worries about exerting yourself into a heart attack; if you can go up three flights of stairs, you can cope with sex.

Numbness after strokes or neurological problems such as paralysis are serious handicaps to a sex life, though not a death-blow. Even if you (female or male) have lost sensation in the genital region, you may not have lost sexual desire. Though you may have lost the ability to get an erection or to climax, your partner may still have needs that, unfulfilled, will put a strain on your relationship. Allowing intercourse although you yourself get nothing from the experience is a selfless way of giving to your partner (usually male in these circumstances). Equally, your partner may need to be told that you, as a woman, still desire sexual stimulation in circumstances where they are unable to provide it; this could be orally, manually, or with artificial aids such as vibrators.

Masturbation

This remains one of the taboos of the age, which is very odd when really we all know that it is common, widely enjoyed, harmless and satisfying – quite apart from being cheap, quick and calling for no long term commitment other than to someone who is already one of your favourite people. This is not meant to be flippant; just how many people, female and male, find masturbation an outlet for their libido who would otherwise lead a sexless life? Someone used to regular sex who loses their partner through illness or misfortune is unlikely to be able to abandon their sexual desire or adopt a life of celibacy.

This could lead to a rather pathetic search for sexual partners, or a demeaning promiscuity, a furtive search for available sex. Or just a lingering regret at the lack of a sexual outlet. Between partners, masturbation may be the only possible way of maintaining a sexual life where illness and disability preclude actual intercourse, despite the measures considered earlier. As with so much else in sexual matters, it is a question of openness, of recognising that desires alter, that libido may wane in one and persist or even increase in another, that desire is valid and does not expire with time. Institutions, too, need to recognise that a sexual life is normal, not an aberration, and that sexual desire is not dirty.

And affection . . .

When the fires are cold, when arthritis limits you to pages 1–12 of the Kama Sutra, when deciding between a cup of coffee or a tumble in bed poses a real dilemma, when the thought of sex sends you both into giggles, something still remains. That something is affection, none the less important for perhaps being celibate. Arguably, this is the real sexual expression when all else has failed; a touch, a hug, saying how you feel, exchanging a glance. This is what keeps relationships going long after other physical expressions have become impossible or have lost their importance, outweighing bickering, disagreements and the travails of life later or otherwise.

Even in our tolerant society, expressions of affection are more socially acceptable than expressions with sexual overtones. This applies more within your family than among friends and acquaintances, who can be expected to take a more liberal, less emotionally contaminated view of sexual relationships continuing into later life. As you get older, express your affections more; it is a truism that life's uncertainty may tomorrow render enduringly precious yesterday's fleeting caress. Similarly, the guilt of love unexpressed may never fade.

Warning symptoms (genito-urinary)

The following should be taken seriously and discussed with your doctor.

Women

- Vaginal bleeding after the menopause, even a minor amount
- A feeling of a constantly full bladder or pressure on the bladder
- Blood in the urine
- A constant vaginal discharge
- Pain on intercourse, especially deep inside
- Any sore area on the vagina that does not heal within a few days.

Men

- Blood in the urine
- Complete loss of erection
- Swelling on the testicles.

Grooming and appearance

How nice it would be to reach retirement looking fair, fit and firm. Unfortunately, you are more likely to be flabby, folded and frazzled. Do not despair; especially, do not give up and, even more especially, do not think that appearance no longer matters once past a certain age.

Fashion, looking smart, taking care of yourself; however you call it, there is a core of importance buried beneath the fashionable flimflammery that we all mock. Who can look at a peacock displaying his finery without being impressed? Or see stags strutting their stuff in proud self-absorption, watching the females out of the corner of their eyes?

The biology of grooming

Display is a feature of life deeply set within our make-up. Much of it has to do with sexual prowess, signalling the biggest, the fittest, the most alluring, even the most idle – all of which implies 'Hey, I'd be a great partner to have babies with; just look at these hips, these shoulders, how well off I am' – you know the rest. Even though sexual allure may no longer be relevant at your age, there remains the satisfaction that we are programmed to register when someone looks at us approvingly and compliments our appearance. Nor is there any reason why this feeling should stop at some arbitrary age, 60, 70, even 80; we do not shed these inherent traits in line with the calendar.

Grooming is clothes, certainly: keeping them clean, co-ordinated and vaguely in fashion. Possibly not completely up to date (because by the third time you see bell-bottomed trousers in fashion, you just *know* you don't want to get into them). But a gesture towards the current look will not go amiss; at least it may establish some credibility with grandchildren. Grooming extends to personal hygiene and appearance. This is really very important as you get older, and not just for the obvious reasons of 'looking neat'. Why does nature make us so aware of grooming and our appearance? It carries a health message. It is important to keep skin clean; this reduces the chances of infections, ulcers and unpleasant smells. It leads you to scrutinise your skin, spotting a mole that looks unusual, or an area of persistently crusted skin that does not heal.

You pay attention to your feet, paring nails, rubbing away hard skin; again, you spot early changes of ulceration, an ingrowing toenail, numbness or discolouration of the toes which could signify poor blood flow.

You run your fingers over your abdomen, breasts and legs, feeling lumps or irregularities; most will be innocent or of no importance but without this regular 'maintenance check' you might overlook a hernia, abdominal swelling of uncertain cause, or an early breast problem.

You look at your eyes and your mouth. Is that a bit yellow? What is that ulcerated area that refuses to heal? Should you get something done about that tooth?

It all comes down to body awareness. If this is how you prefer to regard grooming, then fine, look at it less for its own sake than as a kind of safety check that you run on your body at regular intervals. This may sound obvious; after a certain age the value of this should be obvious, though there is a line to be trodden between self-awareness and self-obsession. In a way, doing regular checks guards against obsession, because you get used to the feel of your own body and this makes it more likely that you will spot a variation sooner rather than later.

The psychology of grooming

So there are good, biological reasons for grooming in terms of disease detection. That surely does not explain shoulder pads and pashminas, or Chelsea boots, Saville Row suits and deconstructed jackets. There is a whole psychology to clothes that we subconsciously understand but less often discuss. Clothes signal status; they say, 'I can afford this label, or this is where I shop.' Resist it as you may, this inevitably sends signals to others looking at you; it allows them to categorise you as to income bracket, social group, attitude of mind, probable other interests – even occupation. You may not like this, you may feel it is materialistic or superficial and so it is, taken to extremes, but the whole of recorded history goes against you – the ornaments, the clothes, the make-up.

We need to categorise people quickly and we do this all the time by picking up on cues, of which clothes and appearance are important aspects, as well as accent, stance, tone of voice and context of meeting. Why should this be? Our biology makes us uncomfortable with strangers, wary and even suspicious; this is nothing to do with being anti-social, it is a self-preservation mechanism which urges caution before abandoning defences. You, who no longer live in a cave but in Guildford or Nottingham, may query the relevance of this but you cannot escape the biological urges that introduce some tension into meetings with strangers.

In addition, appearance helps to signal membership of a group; friends tend to be similar in a number of ways, including grooming and fashionability. How easy it is to deride, as we all have, 'ladies who lunch' with their interchangeable suits, hair-dos and cosmetics, or watched groups of young media people all artlessly showing off their expensive dressed-down uniforms. And yet, within the group, common patterns of dress and grooming send signals that 'we are together'.

There is no reason why this should end at a certain age, any more than the biological undertones should finish at the age of 60. Looking smart, dressing to whatever status you hold – this all goes to project an image that can only enhance how you feel about yourself. Within that image you will choose what you want to project, whether it be smart casual, sleek groomed or relaxed. Nothing could be worse than adopting a dishevelled, unco-ordinated appearance that says to others, 'I've lost it, I don't care. Oh, and my mind is disorganised too.' Because this too is a stereotype (sorry, there is no escaping them) – a stereotype of the neglectful older person who takes so little account of themselves that there is no reason why others should take any account of them either.

Making yourself over

This can be great fun – if your psychology allows it. In leaving work you enter uncertain territory; you are abandoning a context of employment and dress that has been your uniform for many years, shaping people's expectations about the type of person you are. How tempting it can be to make yourself over, remodelling yourself, as it were, in an image that you have chosen, which may be very different from your usual one. You might throw out your wardrobe and start afresh, change your hairstyle, have teeth capped, change glasses. It does not take much to transform your appearance and with it, as we have previously argued, your manner and modes of behaviour. You can easily find colour consultants, personal shoppers or just a trusted friend to guide you towards the new you.

Some things to bear in mind:

- Do not go beyond what your social circle can tolerate; a move from Gap to Gucci may alienate or embarrass your friends.
- Keep things in proportion; dressing like a million dollars while living in a modest apartment invites ridicule.
- Prepare for reality; changing your image might appeal as a fresh

start, but you may be devastated to realise that, underneath, you are still you.

• Keep it fun, or else risk turning into an object of fun.

Dressing for age

As you get older, there are common-sense measures to bear in mind when shopping.

• Get clothes that require minimal effort to clean and are non-iron.
• Avoid things with fiddly hooks and clasps; your fingers will get stiffer and you will find it harder to reach behind you; zips are better.
• Shoes should be secure and not slip or twist over easily; you might prefer slip-ons with Velcro fastenings rather than laces or buckles.
• Think of clothes that mix and match easily so that you look different just by changing a tie, a scarf or an accessory.
• As you get older, staying warm can be a problem. Solve this by dressing in layers; vest, shirt/blouse, a couple of thin sweaters and perhaps a cardigan or fleece will be warmer than two thick sweaters.
• Clean clothes regularly; nothing looks worse than stained, smelly trousers or dresses; this implies that you can't be bothered and tells others not to bother either.

Cosmetic surgery

Here is another technology that is moving from risqué to routine as people – men as much as women – decide that if they can do something about their appearance then they should do it. At the same time a shift in society's attitudes has come to regard what was once bizarre as acceptable. Here are some pros and cons.

Pros

• You choose your appearance
• You gain self-esteem

- You project a more youthful image
- You feel fitter.

Cons

- There is a surgical risk
- It is costly
- Results may be imperfect and temporary
- You will be teased!

Plastic surgery should never be gone into without careful consideration of the risks and benefits. Start by seeing a recommended plastic surgeon – be wary of clinics that advertise themselves; though many are perfectly professional, they will naturally oversell procedures and play down drawbacks. You should satisfy yourself about your surgeon's qualifications, the risks of the procedure, the recovery period, the final appearance and the effects of complications. If you can, let your doctor refer you to a reputable surgeon, though many doctors are reluctant to get involved in this.

It is important to be clear about your expectations of surgery, something which reputable surgeons will explore carefully with you. Some procedures are obviously of benefit, for example the removal of unsightly veins or scars. Others, such as facelifts or nose remodelling, may be part of a search for a transformed you, something which no surgeon can promise. Once the scars have settled and the bruising has gone, you may be disappointed to see that your new appearance has not transformed your social life or improved your personality.

That said, there are plenty of older people who feel and act younger than their biological age and are resentful at looking older than they feel. In such cases, cosmetic surgery can be money very well spent, and certainly less boring than an annuity or a stair lift!

Operations

These can be divided into minor and major, though the division is a bit arbitrary.

Minor
Lip enhancement/wrinkle clearing
This is done by injecting silicon or a similar substance under the skin or into the lips, making the area fuller and so enhancing the appearance and disguising wrinkles. Another method is to inject a drug (botulinum toxin) which makes muscles relax, so smoothing out wrinkles.

For: Low risk and immediate effect.

Against: Usually temporary; surgery is immediately obvious.

Destroying thread veins/varicose veins
Small veins are destroyed using electro-cauterisation, a fine needle, to obliterate the blood vessels responsible. Varicose veins – which are just normal veins that have lost the surrounding support which keeps them straight – can be removed by injecting a substance into the vein that makes the walls stick together, tying off feeder veins or, more ambitiously, stripping out the vein.

For: Relatively safe with predictable outcome.

Against: Temporary, some scarring.

Hair implants
Clumps of hairs are transplanted from the back of the head to the front and eventually take root.

For: Effective, reliable results.

Against: Takes time, looks obvious; there is a risk of scarring.

Tattoo removal/skin blemishes
Laser vaporisation has greatly improved the efficiency of dealing with these unwanted legacies of your past.

For: A relatively straightforward procedure.

Against: The skin often looks unnatural; risk of scarring often outweighs benefit of removing minor skin blemishes.

Major
Face lift/eye lid lift
Aged skin loses its elasticity, sagging and going baggy especially under the eyes and under the chin. The operation lifts the loose skin off the underlying tissue and pulls it back towards the scalp, where the scars are unobtrusive. Surplus skin is trimmed away. The eye-lift

185

is less extensive and can be done under local anaesthetic.
For: Can transform your appearance, especially around the eyes.
Against: You look dreadful while recovering, you may have an artificially stretched appearance, and there is a small risk of damage to nerves in the face. The effects are temporary.

Nose surgery
Commonly, procedures are to straighten a nose, remove bumps, or reshape the nose completely. Of less appeal to older people unless the nose is greatly distorted.
For: Small changes have great cosmetic effect.
Against: A small risk of infection; the final appearance is less predictable as you get older.

Liposuction
A rather brutal procedure to vacuum out fat cells from the hips and thighs, for example.
For: Instant remodelling.
Against: Significant risk of infection; final appearance may be dimpled and uneven.

Tucks of abdomen/bottom/arms
These are all variations on a theme of tightening-up drooping skin; it often also involves removing fatty tissue.
For: Improves appearance under clothes.
Against: Temporary effect and gives areas that look obviously artificially tightened.

Breast enhancement/reduction
Changes to fatty tissues and post-menopausal loss of support often leave women with breasts that are pendulous or look withered. Large breasts can cause significant neck and back pains. Either can be helped by removing fatty tissue or implanting sacs.

The safety of implants has been under question; most doctors feel that the risks have been greatly exaggerated.
For: Usually very satisfying results, enhancing self-esteem.
Against: Risks of loss of sensation; breast enhancement gives an appearance obviously inconsistent with your age.

Case study

Both Mary and her partner Peter led active lives in retirement. In their mid-60s, their routine included golf, aerobics and walking; they did not smoke and ate healthily. Despite this, both were disappointed to look at themselves in a mirror, seeing sagging chins, loose eyelids and many skin blemishes and moles. No matter how smartly they dressed or how well they held themselves, they felt that their physical appearance was sapping their mental youthfulness. They were embarrassed to talk about this to their acquaintances but, when they did so, found that several were feeling the same and were considering plastic surgery. Everyone seemed to know someone who had had something done, though no one admitted to surgery on themselves.

Between their friends they came up with the names of several apparently reputable plastic surgeons. They discussed things with their GP, who was able to check on the qualifications of the surgeons and who had patients who had been well treated by a couple of them. Their GP did not think it was at all odd that they were considering surgery, though he cautioned about expecting it to transform their lives.

They visited two clinics to discuss the options. The first was very enthusiastic about what could be done and suggested a number of tucks and tweaks that would enhance their appearance, including liposuction on Mary's hips, which she had not considered. They seemed professional and honest and had an easy payment scheme. The second clinic was less enthusiastic about possible procedures and spent as much time talking about Mary and Peter's expectations as about surgery. The clinic had a wide collection of before and after photos for Mary and Peter to study.

They found it difficult to decide between the two clinics. In the end Peter opted for the first clinic, preferring their businesslike approach, and had bags removed from under his eyes and several moles cut off. He was delighted with the procedure and ended up exactly as he expected. Mary opted for the second clinic; it suited her to spend a lot of time discussing her motivation for plastic surgery and the likely outcome with a counsellor. In the end she opted for a face-lift, and injections to relieve wrinkles. The clinic actually dissuaded her from having liposuction ('wear trousers') and from a tummy tuck ('your abdominal muscles are too lax for you to benefit'). She too was pleased with the outcome and appreciated the relaxed and sympathetic guidance she had received on her choice of procedures.

> *I don't wish to be everything to everyone but I do wish to be something to someone.*
>
> Unknown

11

How to Be Fulfilled
Yet Avoid Guilt

Things past redress are now with me past care.

Shakespeare, *Richard II*

You want your retirement to be fun and as unencumbered as possible, and to run your life as you want. Plenty of people will try to bully you and make you feel guilty about this, sometimes with justification, often not. This chapter is to prepare you for the common sources of guilt and suggest ways of dealing with them. Not that you should feel so bad about guilt; a little bit of guilt will get you up in the morning, make you mow the lawn, think about decorating, nudge you towards developing new interests, keep you in touch with family and tell your partner what a great job they are doing in coping with you.

Guilt in small doses is motivating but too much is bad.

- It paralyses action
- Then it tends to favour quick fixes that are unsatisfactory long-term solutions
- It disturbs sleep
- It is often incapable of completely satisfactory solution
- It spoils enjoyment

- You don't get thanks for doing the right thing.

The additional downside of guilt is that it threatens your belief in yourself and makes your self-confidence wobbly, something it shares with other strong emotions. Fortunately, as you get older your sense of your own worth becomes stronger, making you rather more resistant to guilt than when younger. If allowed to go too far this could become indifference, a trait which is as unattractive in the old as it is in the young. You should try to be aware of that happy mixture of prioritising your own needs without disregarding the legitimate claims of others. Those others are, in order of accessibility, your partner, your family (including parents), friends, colleagues and public and official organisations, especially the government.

In this chapter we shall look first at some common post-retirement situations that generate guilt, reasons why others might want to make you feel guilty, and how to handle them.

Common situations arousing guilt

You're being selfish . . .

The charge
You spend all day at the golf club/down at the pub/hunched over the computer/on holiday/in the shops. You didn't ask us about your holiday dates; we were hoping you'd babysit that day. Have you made a will yet? Have you made provision for your old age?

The sub-text
We are really busy people doing important things like running the country or learning to make authentic gnocchi. You are an idle old buffer with too much time on your hands, probably too much money and you cannot be trusted to look after yourself or arrange your own affairs. Your time/decisions/planning is unreliable, so you should just do what we suggest.

Oh, and it's just not fair that you can stop for a coffee whenever you want while I have all this economic analysis to do.

The reply
I'm really glad that you think about me and keep my best interests in mind. You know that (x,y,z) is never far from my thought and I'm always glad to know what you are considering. But you should be glad that I have my own interests and plans; otherwise I'd be expecting you to do more for me such as taking me shopping, helping me choose how to redecorate, doing something about the lousy public transport, etc., etc. In fact, since you are so concerned about me, here is a list of things I'd like to do which you could help me with.

You shouldn't do that at your age

The charge
Those clothes look ridiculous on you; whatever happened to that old cardigan? And don't think you can conceal your age by having a face lift. There's no point in going on holiday/to clubs on your own; who is going to look at you? That (man/women/floozy/gold digger) can never replace our (Mum/Dad). You never could drive, so why did you buy that (gleaming/sporty) number?

The sub-text
We used to know where we stood with you; if you start changing things we won't know what to expect. We find it hard to think of you showing affection/building new relationships/having sex at your age; this affects our memories of our Mum/Dad/your previous partners. Why should you have things we can't afford yet?

The reply
My happiness should be your happiness and if that involves change and new relationships you must accept that that is my right. As for sex, spending and new clothes, don't talk like an old man/woman.

You keep asking for help

The charge
You're getting too demanding; we can't cope.

The sub-text

I can see you need more help and support but I have my own
responsibilities too and I cannot be available all the time. I'd help
more but you don't seem appreciative; you take it as your right. I'm
worried about getting too involved because before I know it I will be
a full-time carer and I cannot face that prospect.

The reply

I understand your concerns; I'm no more happy about my situation
than you are, but you are family and I did support you, so I am
entitled to some help now. That said, I do not want to be a burden
for long so let us think constructively about my needs. This may
involve some hard choices, with financial implications, but these
will not go away by ignoring them. I do appreciate your help; I
know I haven't said so enough. Let's try to agree a regular programme
of help to save me calling on you unexpectedly.

Don't squander your assets

The charge

You should look after your money because you'll need it later.

The sub-text

You seem to have plenty of money to do what you want; it's silly to
spend it on things you don't really need. Care in old age is expensive
and we cannot afford it. In any case it would be a pity to see all your
money go on care; there will be none left for us.

The reply

If I have money now it is because I was careful over many years;
otherwise you really would need to pay more for me. While I am
healthy I don't see why I shouldn't enjoy myself to the best of my
ability; I could die tomorrow. Whatever I leave will be taxed anyway.
I would like to leave you money and I'm prepared to discuss with an
adviser whether I can do this while still having enough to live on.

Special situations arousing guilt

Family

Although getting older should bring wisdom and resignation, sometimes it does just the opposite. Tensions established in early life may actually become more important with time – the child who accuses you of always having favoured another, or the child who has been a disappointment but for whom you continue to feel responsible. There may be tensions to do with how your children are bringing up their own children. There are frequently resentments between your own siblings, based on what they have achieved in their lives in terms of careers, status, assets, pensions and health, and this can be a source of aggravation just when you can do without it. Similarly, siblings may blame supposed discrimination in childhood for their current situation.

Remarriage (or finding a new partner)

Though this might appear a feature unique to our times, thought shows that this is an ancient problem. It is the problem of surrogacy, the subject of dozens of fairy stories and literature, where a step-parent jeopardises the stability of a family and everyone struggles to find mutually acceptable ways of relating to each other. This is not easy; there is absolutely no reason why your children or parents should take to your new partner. Much depends on circumstances – it is somehow easier to accept new relationships when the old one ended through fate (illness, death) rather than through choice (divorce, abandonment). This way the sincerity of your feelings towards the departed can stay unquestioned, even idealised, and with time outsiders can accept your wish to make a new life because that fact does not diminish the worth of your previous one.

Even so, new partners coming into a family can resurrect ancient tensions and you need to tread carefully to avoid raising hackles. Fortunately, most families welcome newcomers, especially in our times when relationships often break down anyway after a few years. But there may never be the warmth that you would like and there may be a suspicion about motives that puts a certain tension into your own relationship.

What can you do about this? Do you want to do anything about this? The following points can help you come to terms with the situation.

- Decide how important good family relationships are to you; do you want to make the effort required?
- Maintain communication – no matter how hard, even if it is just a card at Christmas. You never know when situations may force a rethink on an apparently established confrontation.
- Consider the practical implications – is there an estate to manage, legal responsibility for children, powers of attorney over parents' affairs?
- Little things carry big weight; remembering a birthday can convey more feeling than overlooking a technical affront.
- Focus on what has gone right rather than what has gone wrong, on what has been positive rather than negative.
- Do not rub in differences, this will only cause resentment or envy.
- You have a life; your views, desires and plans are valid; those with whom you have difficulties have their lives too and their goals are not necessarily your goals.
- You cannot solve everything; there will be some issues that are incapable of resolution. Either you make an effort to move on, putting past grievances behind you, or else you must reconcile yourself to enduring angst, confrontation or estrangement. If there is not a best path, choose the least worst.

Money

It is not true that you will inevitably be poor after retirement; older people have increasing economic power and many can look forward to a comfortable retirement, though not necessarily an affluent one. Why should this be? The reasons include inherited assets, especially a parental house, the spread of pension schemes, increased provision for their own retirement, a cushion of state benefits. There are also many opportunities for part-time work.

At the same time, your requirements decrease; if you don't believe this, just make a list of the basic requirements to run your home and car and buy food and utilities (don't forget to allow for tax on income, though). You will be surprised at how small a figure it is now that you no longer have to pay for children, mortgage, commuting, professional fees, insurance, pension funds, etc., etc. Of course this is the cost of just existing; you want more out of life than that, but it is a cheering reminder that you have economic freedom.

You might feel guilty about this, seeing the struggles that your own children are going through – assuming that you retire at or about 60, they will be in their 30s and facing all the overheads you have left behind. How do you cope with this?

- Ensure your own comfort and security – this means making quite sure that your own needs are met for now and for the foreseeable future. You might need professional help to do this, to calculate future income, overheads, a fund for luxuries and emergencies. Only you will know what level you feel comfortable with and you should resist feeling guilty about this – after all, if you do not make provision for yourself, there will be a moral obligation on your family to do so.
- Give away only what you can comfortably afford and only after careful assessment – you might need advice on tax implications.
- It might be better to be open with your family about any plans to give away assets, rather than spring it as a surprise, however pleasant. They may not want help, or not in the form you have in mind; they might, for example, prefer that help goes to their own children, your grandchildren.
- Don't let others tell you what you should live on; do not let others force their stereotype of what you should do in retirement on to you.
- Things will change; as you get older your needs are likely to decrease, as you holiday less, go out less; however, your costs for care may rise. Be prepared to reassess your requirements regularly and try to avoid long-term commitments that look less wise when your own requirements alter.

Friends

Old friends are as good as family, possibly better because the friendship survives by mutual choice rather than the hand of chance. Having been spared the tensions of family life, the relationship is more likely to be based on shared interests and a shared perspective in life and so there is every reason for this to continue after retirement. That said, friendship requires space; certain relationships that work in small quantities do not survive greater exposure. Therefore do not feel aggrieved if friends that you saw only occasionally before retirement seem reluctant to meet more often.

On the other hand, it is quite likely that there are people for whom you never quite had the time to get to know better and paradoxically you may grow closer to these after retiring. Retirement as we have described it should be an opportunity to explore new interests and make new friends. These may be context-specific – people you only see at a golf club, or an evening class. Others may be drawn into your regular social circle and here you need to be aware of the effect on older friends, who may feel that they have a first claim on your friendship.

If they make you feel guilty by remarks such as, 'We don't see as much of you these days; you always seem busy', take it as a compliment that they value your friendship and want it to continue. Quite how you do this depends on your style – you may enjoy parties for the many, having a few words with each, or you may prefer gatherings with just another couple. Your style will determine how to introduce new friends to your old friends, the chances being that your friends will be similar in the ways they like to relate to each other.

The public

In retiring you move from one kind of stereotype, appropriate to your occupation and status, to another, that of the retired older person. People will react to you according to their views on the stereotype of a retired person, just as you react to others based on your own stereotypes. Stereotypes are not as awful as they sound; it makes good sense to categorise the world and the people in it rather than attempt to deal with every passing person as an individual –

you just cannot do it. But, a big but, it is a short step from stereotype to prejudice, the step from probably to definitely. This is what gives stereotypes a bad name.

You need to understand this if you are to cope with the guilt that complete strangers may try to pin on you. Their stereotypes of a retired person may include any or all of the following: time wasters, past it, drags on society, tetchy, pompous, old-fashioned. Note that there need be nothing behind these phrases at all – ask people to explain their stereotypes and you will probably get an incoherent mumble – but they still affect behaviour. So you may be ignored in shops, patronised in restaurants, chivvied along on public transport. People may assume that you are dumb and incapable of understanding modern technology, out of touch with the world. Or they may go to another extreme and assume that you are incapable of taking even small decisions, let alone handling your own affairs – sadly, the caring professions are especially prone to make these assumptions.

Others will target you as easy prey: doorstep sellers, itinerant builders, and dubious financial advisers are the more common of this category.

How are you to cope with this? First, accept that your appearance matters – we have touched on this earlier and it is important. If you dress in a dishevelled way do not be surprised if people assume that your state of mind is similarly disorganised. This is not even a conscious process, as you will realise if you think how you yourself relate to others. It only takes a second to categorise others, just as swiftly as they will categorise you. So look as if you know what you are about. Similarly, try to keep your home and car looking cared for, because this says that you keep an eye on things.

Try to know what you want when buying services; make a list, do a bit of research for more complex issues such as insurance, have a rule about whether you will or will not speak to people who cold call. Best of all, go by previous satisfaction and recommendation. If you feel pressurised into an important decision, learn how to call time out. Useful phrases are: 'I need to discuss this with my family/accountant/lawyer', 'I need time to think this through', 'I don't see why you need such a quick decision; you have to leave it with me'. You might be embarrassed to say the words, but even just running them through your head can strengthen your resolve.

While being prudent, try not to fall into a paranoid view of the world or others. The majority of people selling services are decent and it is not in their interests to force you into an unsuitable choice. Your custom is valuable, increasingly so, and they know that older people are more likely than younger people to be loyal to organisations that have served them well in the past

Voluntary organisations

Many of these will see you as fair game to participate in their activities. Elsewhere I have argued just how useful this can be, not just for the work these organisations do, but in terms of your own self-esteem and enjoyment. The range is enormous – religious organisations, meals on wheels, teaching others, befriending families; if you want to do something there will be a niche for you.

But such activities do not appeal to everyone; you might find it positively off-putting to continue dealing with the public if that has been your working life; you might have other plans for how you want to spend your time or other demands on your resources. In these circumstances a diplomatic refusal, whatever it costs in short-term embarrassment, is better than to be whipped into reluctant activity; remember that it is always easier to decline requests by showing that you have alternatives rather than giving a blank no.

It may be that when you retire you want to resign from organisations in order, as it were, to simplify your life. It is sensible to signal your intention well in advance; this lets the organisation plan for your leaving and also allows you to get all the arm twisting of the 'Oh, just another six months please' type out the way. From a psychological aspect, making this sort of decision will stimulate you to consider your plans, whether you want something else to fill the gap or just to take a rest.

Government and official organisations

Like it or not you are bound to have dealings with these in the shape of the tax authorities, local councils, the NHS and Social Services, let alone utilities. Mostly you can expect to be dealt with by conscientious individuals who are trying their best; it's often the official language that is off-putting, but there is a human face behind it. Things can get confusing whatever your age; most organisations have help desks to try to clarify your queries and you need feel no guilt about using these. Write down your query; as well as making sure you cover all important points; this will often clarify your mind about your difficulty. Sources of further advice are the Citizen's Advice Bureau and Age Concern, as well as your usual professional advisers (see the directory of services in Chapter 13).

Many older people feel guilty about calling on the Social Services or the NHS and this is well recognised by those who work in these organisations. Remember that you have contributed to these services through council tax and income tax and are entitled to the appropriate benefits. Advice is free, so professionals can tell you what can be done. Given the financial pressures on these organisations, you will find that there are gaps between what you want and what can be provided, especially in relation to health problems if you require surgery for a hip replacement, for example. You should let your doctor know about any serious deterioration in health problems for which you are on a waiting list, as this may alter your priority for treatment.

It is becoming increasingly common to opt for private treatment for health problems even though you may not have health insurance, paying for the procedure out of savings. This is most commonly done for hip or knee replacements or cataract surgery, procedures for which NHS waiting times are often scandalously long. You should not think of this as jumping a waiting list, rather, it is a use of your resources in your best interests and in order to improve your quality of life. Your doctor can guide you about this.

The guilt of getting older

It is a curious aspect of Western society that the old feel guilty; in many other areas, particularly in the East, the old are venerated and far from being made to feel guilty are treated as still useful members of society. This attitude is easier to maintain in a society of extended families, where several generations live in close proximity, probably in the same house. In these set-ups there is a constant interchange of value which preserves the self-esteem of everyone; the older people give advice about child care, careers, money matters and life in general, based on their own experience, memories and philosophy. The younger members give companionship, help with cleaning, shopping and arranging more complex matters.

These arrangements do still exist, perhaps rather more so than might be imagined from media reports of the 'death of the family', but there is no doubt that they are under strain in modern Britain. The dependency of getting old therefore becomes a self-fulfilling prophecy. Since you cannot cope with shopping, you do have to call on your family, which they may resent. As you are confused, you need their advice; when you need more help, they have to arrange it rather than popping in on you. This all puts a strain on the most caring family and, in recognition of this, you may hesitate to call for help for fear of jeopardising previously good relationships. Though ultimately every family has to find its own path, there are certain principles:

- Most parents deserve help and respect and it is primarily the duty of the family to provide this.
- Be honest about difficulties in order to get outside help (Social Services, for example) at an early stage.
- Once dependent, recovery is unlikely; plan realistically and plan ahead.

The guilt of the survivor

The older you get, the more likely you are to lose loved ones through illness, separation or death; there is a well recognised risk of feeling guilty for still being alive, let alone in good health. This is a uniquely human emotion, reflecting as it does deep attachment to others. In other regards it can oppress your life, tingeing any enjoyment with sadness, possibly even to the point of depression and self-loathing. Fortunately, most older people are wise enough to see disability and death with more philosophical eyes than the young do, but as the distractions of an active life fade you may well find yourself brooding on earlier losses. If this induces depression, you might benefit from medication. Along with that, it is helpful to record the life of others and to talk things through. This is definitely not counselling; this is not an attempt to explain away the emotions or even reconcile you to them. It is means of bringing memories and emotions out on to the surface, but only as far as you choose.

You can be the vessel through which these others survive and through whom their memory is kept alive. It can be desperately sad to perform this function, especially as it has been thrust on you by life. Some find comfort in a religious faith, others through the act of memory and talking itself. What you must try to avoid is feeling guilty about how life has affected others.

If I am not for myself, who will be for me; and if for myself alone, what am I? And if not now, when?

Rabbi Hillel

12

Positive Old Age: How to Cope with the Inevitabilities of Ageing

In three words I can sum up everything I've learned about life: It goes on.
Robert Frost

Successful ageing

This may seem an odd concept; can you really control how you get older? However, studies have shown that there are certain characteristics shared by those whose ageing appears to give them satisfaction and who maintain their faculties longer than most.

How to define successful ageing? There are several components: your state of physical health, your state of mental health, the inevitable effects of age itself and one's own assessment of satisfaction.

Your state of physical health

Physical health is the essential underpinning of satisfaction in later life; to be in constant pain, unable to go out, or read, or hear properly

– these misfortunes will test the most optimistic mental attitude. The evidence is that the most successful agers try to remain active, take regular exercise and keep pushing their bodies to do the best they can, despite disabilities. Elsewhere there are guidelines on diet, exercise and keeping fit.

Bear in mind that exercise is worthwhile at virtually any age; you are never past it. There is a benefit from using your limbs and taking a walk, even though it makes you a little breathless. Swimming suits many older people, because the buoyancy of the water takes the strain off joints, while the warm, moist atmosphere aids breathing. Walking itself can be tailored to suit your mood and abilities, from a gentle stroll to the shops to an energetic ramble. Other options are exercise classes, dancing and aerobics. Or even just making yourself walk upstairs, stretching and swinging your limbs.

It is best to develop a habit of exercise well before retirement; as well as being good for you anyway, it is valuable in setting a pattern that you continue as long as possible. However, it really is never too late; all evidence supports the benefit that comes from taking up exercise for the first time at any age.

Your state of mental health

Those who age most successfully tend to have an optimistic outlook on life; they are more likely to be sociable within recreational groups and religious and communal organisations. It is noticeable that they maintain contact with their families; those who are socially isolated age less well. According to some research, mental alertness and continuing sociability seem better predictors of living long than physical health. So try to stay within society and maintain friendships and socialising for as long as possible.

Unfortunately, a positive outlook cannot overcome serious health problems such as cancer; research does not bear out the widely proclaimed belief that you can conquer it by having the right attitude of mind. However, it is well accepted that depression or anxiety lower the threshold for pain and disability, making unbearable what you could otherwise cope with. Conversely, anti-depressant drugs (in very low doses) are very useful to help chronic pain, through actions on pain pathways that we do not fully understand.

So mental health will not put off ageing, but it will make it feel more tolerable, especially when faced with serious health problems.

Thinking good, feeling good

This may seem another odd, folksy concept. How can thinking about yourself alter the facts of your age and abilities? Surely this is just the much derided 'pull yourself together' concept? It is a pity that popular prejudice has been allowed to devalue the power of positive thinking – because that is exactly what we are talking about. If you think of yourself as old at the age, say, of 60, then you will subconsciously start to act old in ways that reflect your stereotype of elderly behaviour. If you think you have to mollycoddle yourself, you will do so. If you expect to tire easily, find travel aggravating and new experiences daunting and believe that you are incapable of learning, it is hardly surprising if you regress to a wary individual turned in on yourself. Do you really want to mark time in this way for 20 years?

Common experience shows the importance of a positive mental attitude. You can think of individuals who have faced similar difficulties but who have taken quite different attitudes to them. On the one hand there are those who crumble, forever returning to their misfortune and blaming it for all sorts of later problems. At first people sympathise, but sympathy eventually becomes weary and impatient and risks being withdrawn, possibly through fear of being dragged down into a constant scene of self-pity.

Meanwhile others, without in any way dismissing the seriousness of their problem, look for a way to move forward and possibly learn from adverse events. Remarkably, these people find that the strength to do so arises spontaneously from within themselves once they have shaken themselves down mentally. It may be from a religious faith or a philosophical outlook; it doesn't matter. Friends and relations are more likely to sympathise for longer in such cases, feeling that they are contributing to a positive outcome.

Probably you cannot acquire a positive mental attitude, it is a question of your personality and your unique heredity and life experience. It is unrealistic to imagine that you can reinvent yourself psychologically just because you are getting older, yet you will without doubt be faced with difficulties as you get older that will pose a challenge to your mental resilience. You will find that the sympathy of others easily wears thin. We all have our problems and life is endlessly disappointing or unfulfilling; this is so true that we don't actually want to hear it all the time. We want to hear about improvement, happiness, the unexpected, the hopeful and there is every opportunity for these attitudes to persist well past retirement.

The whole package

Therefore, those who age well have a package of characteristics, some within their control, many decided by fate, chance and heredity. How to come to terms with all this is a theme that has taxed the greatest philosophers, playwrights and authors. Nothing you read here can match their musings. But in simple practical terms you can aim for the following:

- Stay involved with people and society
- Maintain interests and interest for as long as you can
- Stay physically active for as long as you can manage it
- Draw your family and community around you.

What to expect as you get older

Physical, mental and social changes

Any realistic book about health after retirement must at least acknowledge the things which can go wrong. We have quite deliberately played down these aspects of ageing, not in order to present a totally rosy picture but because it is a fact that most elderly people stay reasonably well most of the time. This may come as a surprise to those readers who imagine the whole ageing thing to be like a house of cards; one slip and it's total collapse. This is just not true. Of course disability and handicap become more common as you get older, but even by the age of 80 the great majority of people are in adequate health, as defined by their own assessment of disability or ill-health.

However, what sorts of disability should you expect as you get older? Disability is defined as problems with balance, weakness, breathlessness, joint stiffness and lack of co-ordination severe enough to be inconvenient but not reaching the stage of requiring outside support. Major disabilities include Parkinson's disease, arthritis, strokes, blindness and dementia.

About 20 per cent of the age group 65–74 have some degree of disability through these and other causes, most of it mild. Just 0.74 per cent are severely handicapped, under one in a hundred.

About a third of those above 75 have some disability; though only 3 per cent are severely disabled. Even looking to advanced old age, the figures remain fairly reassuring. Of all those over 85s, about a quarter require assistance, with about 18 per cent being confined to their home or an institution.

Parkinson's disease
Overall this affects one or two people in every thousand. This rises to about 2 per cent of those in their 80s.

Strokes
Mini-strokes (also called transient ischaemic attacks or TIAs) are fairly common; the numbers are very difficult to quantify but affect about one in a thousand per annum of people in their 60s onwards. It is typical of a TIA that any paralysis or confusion disappears within about 24 hours.

Major strokes become more likely the older you are, causing paralysis of an arm or leg and affecting speech and comprehension; there is about a 1–2 per cent annual risk in those above the age of 65. Of these many will make a substantial recovery.

Arthritis
Some degree of arthritis of the knees, hips, shoulders or hands is virtually normal by the age of 65, but under 20 per cent of sufferers actually complain of symptoms. Disabling arthritis is much less common.

Blindness
There are about 140,000 registered blind people in the UK and another 100,000 registered as partially sighted. Common causes are cataracts, macular degeneration and glaucoma; less commonly, strokes and injuries.

Dementia

This includes Alzheimer's disease and the effects of strokes, plus various metabolic conditions and alcoholism. Though greatly feared and devastating in its effects dementia is a relatively small risk; it affects 2–3 per cent of those aged 65–75, rising to 20 per cent of the over-80s. The effects can vary from modest confusion but an ability to cope within a constant environment, to total loss of control requiring institutionalisation.

Cancers

Cancer is on the whole age-related, the incidence rising steeply with age. However the broad term cancer conceals a multitude of types of cancer, each with its special characteristics, treatability, disability and relation to age. Here are some examples of the commoner cancers.

Breast cancer

The commonest cancer in women, newly affecting about 0.14 per cent at the age of 45, increasing to 2.4 per cent by the age of 85; these are cumulative risks, so that overall about 6 per cent of women will develop breast cancer at some point in their lives.

Cancer of the womb

Another age-related risk, rising from 0.06 per cent of new cases at the age of 50 to 12.5 per cent at the age of 70. However, unlike breast cancer, the risks fall back after the 70s.

Cancer of the bowel (colon and rectum)

Overall there is a 2 per cent risk of developing one of these cancers, the likelihood increasing from the age of 60 onwards. They are the second commonest cancers in the UK after lung cancer.

Lung cancer

This affects 40,000 people a year in the UK, men more than women, though the relative incidence is changing as smoking patterns change. Men have been smoking less and lung cancer has become less common recently. Women began smoking more a couple of decades ago; the rate of lung cancer is now rising rapidly among women.

Stomach cancer

The third most common (after lung and bowel), affecting 15 in every 100,000 people per year – about 8,000 new cases per annum in the UK.

Prostate cancer

About 14,000 new cases a year and about 9,000 deaths; the second commonest cause of death from cancer in men after lung cancer. Traces of prostate cancer are common if looked for; for example, it is found in one third of men in their 70s, and in two-thirds in their 80s; this is not necessarily life threatening and the optimum treatment for such cancer remains controversial.

Heart disease

Some 1 in 3 of the over-65s have heart disease, showing itself as angina, heart failure, heart valve problems and heart attacks.

Heart disease in one form or another makes up the most common cause of death in the UK, with some 150,000 people dying each year. However, the incidence is falling for reasons that are still controversial. Heart disease includes heart attacks – these account for the great majority of deaths – and heart failure, which is often caused by high blood pressure.

Lung disease

Chronic bronchitis and emphysema, though not often fatal, are important causes of impaired lifestyle through breathlessness. In middle age about 17 per cent of men and 8 per cent of women are affected; for the majority it is not much more than a matter of wheezing and breathlessness on exertion, together with an increased risk of chest infections. Many fewer are disabled by these conditions, though those who are have a very poor quality of life indeed.

Incontinence

Urinary incontinence is common and under-reported; for most people it is only an annoyance but some find it a serious social and personal problem. Figures are difficult to obtain but suggest that about 5 per cent of women in their 60s are affected, 7–8 per cent through the 70s and as many as 25 per cent of women by the age of

85. For men figures are even more elusive: perhaps 2–3 per cent of the very old, and more of those in institutions.

Incontinence of faeces

This is less common, affecting perhaps 3 per cent of all over 65s, though that figure is greatly influenced by the high incidence of faecal incontinence among the very elderly in institutions.

Depression

A common and unsurprising feature of old life, bearing in mind all the changes the elderly have to endure. Depression in the elderly deserves at least as much attention as in younger people. A depressed older person is more at risk of committing suicide, especially if they are isolated, have other significant health problems and drink excessive alcohol. Depression is less easy to spot in an older person; their sadness, loss of appetite, poor sleep or agitation are all too easily attributed to age alone or some upset. Drug treatment is effective at all ages, though dosage needs to be chosen carefully and side effects minimised.

Isolation and social changes

It is frustrating to find that society ignores you, when within yourself you feel as alert as you have ever been; practical difficulties with transport and mobility can render an otherwise lively older person housebound, to their intense irritation. If this is how you find yourself, try to show others that you retain interest and intellect. Have books, magazines, television, computers and hobbies. Otherwise, sadly, helpers and even relatives will quickly stereotype you as 'incapable' and therefore lacking in your faculties. Even professionals can fall easily into this misconception.

Independence and income

It is overwhelmingly likely that you will remain independent well into old age; of all over-65s, under 3 per cent are in institutional care, though this rises to about 25 per cent of the over-85s. In addition, and despite all the various disabilities that you can list on paper, most elderly people regard themselves as reasonably fit and are as active as they choose to be within their limitations.

Economics

There is much confusion about the economic circumstances of the elderly; this may be because we have been in a period of transition from reliance on the state pension and relatively little separate provision for old age, to a situation where occupational pension schemes are widespread. There is also controversy over what is meant by poverty. Economists distinguish between absolute poverty, meaning not having enough money for food, clothing, heat and shelter, and relative poverty, where income is insufficient to provide a lifestyle regarded as the norm by society. There is little doubt that absolute poverty is uncommon in the UK; there is still a decent raft of support to provide care, accommodation and food and this is supplemented by an amazing array of voluntary input. Undeniably there are pockets of severe deprivation; sometimes on analysis these are due to an elderly person choosing an eccentric lifestyle and declining available help. This is a matter of more concern to family and neighbours than it is for the individual themselves.

Relative poverty is a tricky concept to apply to the elderly. Is it poverty not to have electronic games, digital television, visit a burger bar regularly or buy take-away food? The question is clearly absurd put that way, because it assumes that you, post-retirement, will share the economic desires of the rest of the population. You may be quite content to have enough money to get around, have coffee out, visit the cinema and buy a few clothes and have no wish at all to take regular holidays or refurnish your house. Your tastes if retired in your 50s will be different from those in your 60s and 70s. Arguably you will not have retired anyway without calculating your requirements and likely income, unless forced by ill-health or redundancy.

The indications are that many people retire into comfort and enjoy considerable disposable income, together with a substantial asset base. Companies increasingly recognise this and there is a clear 'grey market' that wields considerable economic clout. These affluent retirees enjoy good health, positive attitudes and the means to indulge their wishes in terms of holidays, clothes, pastimes and consumer goods.

Four keys to successful ageing

Ideally you will want to pass your time post-retirement respected by your peers and held in affection by your family and partner. The ways to do so are very simple indeed:

- Keep active physically and mentally
- Try to remain cheerful
- Talk about your life
- Record your thoughts and philosophy.

Or to put it more poetically:

- Choose your genes, eat your beans.
- Take a tot; walk a lot.
- Though snappy, make someone happy.
- Avoid fret, get a pet.
- And use your brain or it will wane.

The value of 'heritage'

It is a wonderful thing to be able to look back over a lifetime and try to distil the lessons you have learned for the benefit of others – you wish! It is a truism that youth has to relearn what age forgets, as we know from our own experience and those of friends and children. Life is indeed the mother of wisdom. Therefore do not expect others to believe, let alone even accept, your distilled wisdom immediately. Rather, this is a project to undertake for your own satisfaction, in the hope that at some time – and you may not know when – your memories will open a window for others. This should not be a maudlin exercise of self-guided counselling. Rather, it is valuable to remember the cultural changes – what you did at school, how you lived, how you dressed, what your aspirations were at different ages.

There is an explosion of interest in genealogy and it is one of the most common reasons why people use the Internet; there must be a reason why we have become so eager to learn more about our forebears and relatives. Could this be in response to a daily life that is ever more alienating and disruptive of relationships?

Genealogy is one thing; reviewing your life is another, possibly less comfortable. This is a totally personal thing; not everyone wants to think about the past and they find it pointless or upsetting. Others find interest in drawing conclusions about their life, possibly in an attempt to come to terms with uncomfortable memories that were suppressed during the years of work. If you choose to review, I suggest that you start in a matter of fact way. Begin by putting papers in order, throwing out junk and reviewing old photos and documents.

Inevitably the process will stimulate memories, but in a controlled fashion; you can stop at any point and you are not doing it for 'therapy' but for practical reasons such as moving home. It's a good idea anyway to get your documents in order. You will almost certainly be surprised at how the passage of time robs ancient feuds of their power or re-awakens old affections. This is true of the people you swore you'd never speak to again as much as those from whom you simply drifted apart. You might end a session wishing to drop a line to someone or make a phone call to a person you have had no contact with for years.

If you find things upsetting, try to think why; it could be that these are emotions you have long buried but which evidently retain power. Or it could be that there is some lingering guilt or regret that kept the thought out of your consciousness. Even if this process does not lead you to contact others, it may still be useful in getting thoughts and emotions in order, a kind of mental spring-cleaning.

Moving home and changes of circumstance

These events are the most likely to be upsetting and to stimulate old memories, as might be expected. You may be making the change reluctantly through a fall in income, frailty, or other such 'practical grounds'. How hard it is to leave a home of 20, 30, or 40 years and all its accumulated memories. Chances are that where you are going there will be less room, so forcing you to choose which possessions, and therefore memories, you are going to discard. No wonder people put off moving beyond the point of logic; it is such a painful prospect. However, as with so many apparently difficult decisions of later life, there is little to be gained by worrying about the prospect. It is better to get down to the task in the expectation that any initial upset will rapidly fade, faced with the inevitability of having to make choices.

Case study

Martha and Edward had reached their mid-eighties, still independent and still generally able to look after themselves. They had family nearby who visited regularly; they themselves were becoming increasingly reluctant to travel far through feeling unsteady and apprehensive about traffic. They had enjoyed many years of retirement and had travelled widely throughout their 60s and 70s but were now content simply to pass their time at home or visit local shops. Edward's memory was deteriorating and he needed reminding about many day-to-day matters, including a range of medication he took for arthritis and angina. However, he could still cope with cooking and food preparation and enjoyed reading and television. He talked over old times with the local friends they still had and especially with his grandchildren, now in their teens.

They had accepted a home help for cleaning and shopping. Though they had to pay for this, their other expenditure was now so low that they could readily afford this, as well as ensuring that their home was maintained and heated. Martha was more active physically and mentally but felt increasingly obliged to stay home to keep an eye on her husband. This was frustrating for her; she had made enquiries about day centres for Edward, giving her the chance to go out. Also they acquired a cat for companionship and something to care for, though still a pet with a lot of self-reliance.

Every day they made an effort to go out for a walk; if not possible, they practised stretching and breathing exercises, at first with some self-consciousness and feeling slightly foolish. It soon became part of their routine.

Their meals were simple; they tried to have fruit and vegetables daily and were not too obsessed about fatty foods. They drank alcohol most days – a sherry, some wine, a beer, a relatively inexpensive, healthy pleasure.

Martha was increasingly reliant on her children to organise their finances and to research plans for their later care; this was causing some tensions as her children were in their 60s, were themselves retired and had hobbies and travel plans of their own. This made for some difficult conversations and some guilt about calling on them. Nevertheless all saw the benefit of preserving Martha and Edward's independence as long as possible for both their self-esteem and to preserve capital assets – no small consideration.

Martha, and to a lesser extent Edward, had a small but constant worry about suddenly falling seriously ill or having an accident, sudden disability and death. They saw this happening all the time with friends and family. At times the losses were overwhelming and left them depressed, but they had a faith of sorts and soon recovered from any sadness. In anticipation of their own deaths they had long ago put their affairs in order and sorted out many mementoes and possessions. This could have been morbid but in fact had been great fun, going through old photos and old papers with their family.

Their time-scale was no longer years but months and weeks. They had no difficulty with this as their interests had on the whole reduced to just a few weeks ahead, though they did still plan holidays further in advance. They could not avoid some anxiety in their lives but in general they felt they had done very well indeed and would take the future as it came in reasonable contentment.

Though much is taken, much abides; and though we are not now that strength which in old days moved earth and heaven; that which we are, we are.

Tennyson, *Ulysses*

13

Conclusions and Sources of Help

The secret of health for both mind and body is not to mourn for the past, not to worry about the future, or not to anticipate troubles, but to live the present moment wisely and earnestly.

The Buddha

While recognising the basic truth of this, I would add to it the need to look ahead and plan. Our complex society demands such prudence; it is no longer a society where things can be left to happen without making some effort to shape your destiny – in health, finances, social arrangements and housing. I hope I have shown that the process of planning can be stimulating in itself, leading you to explore your potential and encouraging you to clarify your aspirations in life.

Planning leads you away from set modes of thinking and from stereotypes of how you should spend the rest of your life. As I have said in many places, not everyone will find planning congenial or even necessary. You may be one of those people, apparently charmed, whose lives just somehow work out without effort and forethought. Would that the rest of us were like this, but the reality is different for the great majority of us. For those I say:

- Cheat fate by planning ahead
- Stay fresh by exploring life and your capabilities
- Preserve health by living in moderation
- Stay happy by cherishing yourself and your loved ones
- Respect yourself to encourage respect from others.

Add to this some daily exercise, alcohol in moderation, perhaps a pet animal and here is a recipe to make the life you deserve rather than simply marking time. Enjoy.

Further information and advice

Many organisations now exist to help and advise older people; the following list is a selection.

National

UK

Age Concern England
Astral House
1268 London Road
London
SW16 4ER
Tel (information): 0800 731 4931
Web: www.ace.org.uk

Alzheimer's Disease Society
Gordon House
10 Greencoat Place
London
SW1P 1PH
Tel (helpline): 0845 300 0336 (calls charged at local rate)
Web: www.alzheimers.org.uk

The Association of Crossroads Care Attendant Schemes Ltd
10 Regent Place
Rugby
Warwickshire
CV21 2PN
Tel: 01788 573653

Crossroads is a charity offering practical help to carers.

Disability Information Trust
Mary Marlborough Centre
Nuffield Orthopaedic Centre
Headington
Oxford
OX3 7LD
Tel: 01865 227592
Web: www.home.btconnect.com/ditrust/home.htm

The Trust assesses and tests disability equipment and offers advice on products to assist in daily living, from leisure, employment and gardening to arthritic aids, wheelchairs, home adaptations and hoists.

Disabled Living Foundation
380–384 Harrow Road
London
W9 2HU
Tel (helpline): 0870 603 9177
Web: www.dlf.org.uk

Advice on disability equipment.

Help the Aged
St James Walk
London
EC1R OBE
Tel (senior line): 0808 800 6565
Web: www.helptheaged.org.uk

Help the Aged provides practical support to help older people live independent lives

The Stroke Association
Stroke House
123–127 Whitecross Street
London
EC1Y 8JJ
Tel: 020 7566 0300
Web: www.stroke.org.uk

Advice and support for sufferers from a stroke and their families.

University of the Third Age – U3A
26 Harrison Street
London
WC1H 8JG
Tel: 020 7837 8838
Web: www.u3a.org.uk

The University of the Third Age assists older people to share educational, creative and leisure activities. U3A members organise their own activities, share their knowledge and experience and develop by learning from other members. Anyone in the Third Age can join U3A – you just need interest and enthusiasm. No qualifications are required and none are given.

Samaritans (Head office)
10 The Grove
Slough
SL1 1QP
Tel (helpline): 08457 90 90 90
Tel (admin): 01753 216500
Web: www.samaritans.org.uk

The Samaritans offer help to people in distress who feel they cannot cope and who may even be considering suicide. Most larger towns have a local branch of the Samaritans; telephone numbers are widely advertised or can be found in the local telephone directory.

Health Information Service
Tel: Freephone 0800 66 55 44

A national freephone network set up by the NHS to help individuals take better care of themselves and know more about health services and their healthcare choices. It is confidential. The service can provide information on a range of health-related topics including:

- How to lead a healthy life
- Self-help and support groups
- Medical conditions and treatments
- How and where to get treatment
- Hospital waiting times
- Medical procedures
- Your rights as a patient.

Keep Fit Association (KFA)
Francis House
Francis Street
London
SW1P 1DE
Tel: 020 7233 8898

The Keep Fit Association offers fitness through movement, dance and exercise. It includes advice and classes for people with disabilities.

National Association of Citizens Advice Bureaux
Myddelton House
115 Pentonville Road
London
N1 9LZ
Tel (National CAB Office): 020 7833 2181
Web: www.nacab.org.uk

For free advice and information on a wide range of issues. Local branches are listed in telephone directories.

Retired And Senior Volunteer Programme (RSVP)
237 Pentonville Road
London
N1 9NJ
Tel: 020 7278 6601

RSVP is part of Community Service Volunteers and believes that retired people form a vast pool of experience and ability. RSVP membership is free and open to anyone senior in age. They will put you in touch with organisations that could benefit from your skills and abilities.

International

Australia

Council on the Ageing (COTA)
Level 2
3 Bowen Crescent
Melbourne, Vic 3004
Tel: (03) 9820 2655
Fax: (03) 9820 9886
E-mail: cota@cota.org.au
Web: www.home.vicnet.net.au/~cotaa/

Council on the Ageing protects and promotes the well-being of all older people. It is an independent consumer organisation run by and for older Australians.

Canada

Division of Aging and Seniors
Population Health Directorate
Health Canada
Address Locator 1908A1
Ottawa, Ontario
KIA 1B4
Tel: (613) 952-7606
Fax: (613) 957-7627
Web: www.hc-sc.gc.ca/seniors-aines

The Division of Aging and Seniors has a well laid out website with links on general health, healthy living and government programmes etc.

USA

Administration on Aging
330 Independence Avenue, SW
Washington, DC 20201
Tel: (202) 619-7501
Fax: (202) 260-1012
E-mail: aoainfo@aoa.gov

A large US Government agency for seniors with many useful links and resources, national and international, on health, taxation, volunteering and work opportunities.

American Association of Retired Persons (AARP)
601 E St. NW
Washington, DC 20049
Tel: 1-800-424-341
E-mail: member@aarp.org

Another large collection of resources for the over 50s with information similar to the above.

Index

men and 171–5
women and 175–6
income, independence and 209–10
incontinence 108, 208–9
independence, income and 209–10
indigestion, self-help and 137–8
information, reliability and 44
insight 75–6
insomnia *see* sleep
intercourse
    frequency of 168–9
    see also sex
interests
    developing new 53–69
    maintaining 157–8
    myths about new 67–8
    previous 53–8
internet 64–5, 162–3, 211
iron 117–18
isolation 209

job, as definition of self 17–18
joints 109
    pains in 135

kidneys 105–6

laxatives, self-help and 138–9
learning
    difficulties in 67
    maintaining 153–66
    memory and 81–6
    task-specific 82
leisure 157–8
libido 168
lip enhancement 185
liposuction 186
losing touch 95–8
loss, and bereavement 149
love, and separation 95–6
lovers 87–9
lungs 105
    cancer 207
    checks on 133–4
    disease 208
    seeking help 142
    warning signs 142

make-overs 182–3

Maslow, Abraham 26
masturbation 178
maturity, skills of 70–86
meal planning 125
medical help, and bereavement 150
memory
    learning and 81–6
    maintaining 153–66
    recording 160–1
men
    impotence and 171–5
    sexual changes with age 170–1
mental ability 110–11
mental activity 163–4
mental health 203–4
mental stability, as goal 49
metabolism 102–3
middle-age spread 123
mind 99–114
    maintenance of 114–52
    senses and 155–9
minerals 118–19
mitochondria 101
molecules of body, changes in 101
money 41
    guilt and 194–5
muscles, 102
    warning signs 143
MUSE, male impotence and 174
myths, new interests and 67–8

nail trimming 141
needs 26–9, 29
    assessment 27
    unmet 129
nervous system
    failure, autonomic 106–7
    warning signs 143
neurological problems, male
    impotence and 173
new experiences, coping with 60–1
new interests
    developing 53–69
    myths about 67–8
nose surgery 186
nutritional needs 117–19

obesity 124
official organisations, guilt and 198–9